Shamanic and Mythic Cultures of Ethnic Peoples in Northern China I

On the basis of first-hand materials gathered through decades of field research and fleshed out with the author's insightful religious, cultural, and historical observations extending back to the Qing dynasty, ancient archaeological discoveries, and the legacy of Siberian peoples, this two-volume ethnological study investigates shamanic rituals, myths, and lore in northern China and explores the common ideology underlying the origins of the region's cultures.

Drawing from numerous oral myths, ancient documents, and archaeological findings, this first volume discusses the spiritual world of northern shamanism and investigates the various rituals, including ancestor worship, fertility, nature deities, blood sacrifice and rites, the worshiping of nature, and shrines. The book illuminates how these rituals and worships, animism, and ideas of the soul are imbedded in and interweave with the indigenous environment, culture, and history of the clans and people of northern China.

The book will be of great value to scholars of religion and to both anthropologists and ethnologists in the fields of shamanism studies, Northeast Asian folklore, and Manchu studies.

Fu Yuguang, a native Manchu scholar of shamanic and Manchu studies from the Jilin Institute for Ethnology, has been committed to ethnological and anthropological research on the myths, rituals, and cultures of Altaic peoples in northern China for over fifty years and has published many influential works.

China Perspectives

The *China Perspectives* series focuses on translating and publishing works by leading Chinese scholars, writing about both global topics and China-related themes. It covers humanities & social sciences, education, media and psychology, as well as many interdisciplinary themes.

This is the first time any of these books have been published in English for international readers. The series aims to put forward a Chinese perspective, give insights into cutting-edge academic thinking in China, and inspire researchers globally.

To submit proposals, please contact the Taylor & Francis Publisher for China Publishing Programme, Lian Sun (Lian.Sun@informa.com).

Titles in history currently include:

The History of Chinese Feudal Society
Tung-tsu Chu

Contemporary Studies on Modern Chinese History I
Zeng Yeying

Contemporary Studies on Modern Chinese History II
Zeng Yeying

Shamanic and Mythic Cultures of Ethnic Peoples in Northern China I
Shamanic Deities and Rituals
Fu Yuguang

Shamanic and Mythic Cultures of Ethnic Peoples in Northern China II
Shamanic Divination, Myths, and Idols
Fu Yuguang

For more information, please visit www.routledge.com/China-Perspectives/book-series/CPH

Shamanic and Mythic Cultures of Ethnic Peoples in Northern China I

Shamanic Deities and Rituals

Fu Yuguang

Translated by Liang Yanjun and Liu Ying

Revised by Daniel A. Kister

Routledge
Taylor & Francis Group
LONDON AND NEW YORK

The publication of this book is sponsored by Ministry of Education of PRC.

First published in English 2021
by Routledge
2 Park Square, Milton Park, Abingdon, Oxon OX14 4RN

and by Routledge
52 Vanderbilt Avenue, New York, NY 10017

Routledge is an imprint of the Taylor & Francis Group, an informa business

English Version by permission of The Commercial Press.

British Library Cataloguing-in-Publication Data
A catalogue record for this book is available from the British Library

Library of Congress Cataloging-in-Publication Data
A catalog record for this book has been requested

ISBN: 978-0-367-65412-2 (hbk)
ISBN: 978-1-003-13251-6 (ebk)

Typeset in Times New Roman
by Apex CoVantage, LLC

Contents

Author's preface and acknowledgements

How time flies! For more than sixty years, I have been dedicated to rescuing, organizing, and studying the precious shamanic cultural legacy that has been passed down among the Altaic peoples over several thousand years. Thanks to the persistent and arduous efforts of like-minded scholars, Chinese ethnic studies and shamanic culture studies have reached out to the world. I have been fortunate to establish connections with many accomplished foreign scholars and academic societies of shamanic studies, which have helped expand my scholarly horizons, bolster my understanding, and nurture deeper insights into the study of Chinese ethnic peoples and shamanic culture. In the past few decades, some of my works and papers in these areas have been translated or introduced to academia in Korea, Japan, Russia, Finland, Germany, Italy, the United Kingdom, and the United States; and several scholars have written to learn more about obscure points of folk customs and phenomena and have expressed hopes of reading original works in this area. With the help of Professor Daniel A. Kister, Professor Liang Yanjun (梁艳君), and Liang Yanjun's fellow translators Wu Chunxiao (吴春晓) and Liu Ying (刘莹, Dalian Polytechnic University), my first Chinese work, *Shamanism and Mythology* (萨满教与神话), published in 1990, has now been translated into English, under the title *Shamanic and Mythic Cultures of Ethnic Peoples in Northern China*. It is my honour, moreover, to have had respected scholar and my good friend Mihály Hoppál take an interest in my work and encourage the publication of this work in English.

I am proficient in the almost extinct Manchu language because I grew up in a family in which the elders spoke Manchu. In 1980, I was assigned to a provincial research unit and threw myself into exploring, rescuing, and investigating the ethnic cultural heritage and traditional folk customs of the Manchu and other peoples of the endangered Altaic language family. I love Manchu history and culture so much so that I easily fitted in with ethnic groups. For more than ten years, I lived in ethnic villages, eating, working, singing, and dancing with the people, and many respected male and female shamans became my bosom friends. I learned to sing sacred chants, seek out holy objects of wood and stone in the mountains, make spirit idols, and beat the drum for sacrificial events. All this impressed me and moved me to collect my findings and publish *Shamanism and Myth*. At that time, shamanism was seen as a backwards superstition and so was banned by the government, but this book took a fresh, positive approach. Bringing to public attention the mystique of northern shamanic culture, it described how shamans serve local people who have no access to modern medical treatment by using traditional herbs and practices to treat disease; it brought to light the time-honoured northern creation myth "War in Heaven" and the ancient traditions of inspired shamanic utterances and divination; it aimed to show that shamans are hardworking, trustworthy masters of clan survival, peace, and harmony.

Throughout the years, I have forged lasting friendships with elders from various ethnic peoples who share a strong belief in their shamanic culture. Now I am greatly indebted to the translators, who have spared no effort in working to make the customs, practices, and idioms of that culture easy for English speakers to the world to understand and appreciate. I think a poem by the famous Tang poet Wang Zi'an (王子安) best expresses my feelings: "A bosom friend afar brings distance near."

Fu Yuguang
October 2019
Changchun

Author's profile

Fu Yuguang (富育光) was born on May 4, 1933, into a Manchu family in Aihui County, present Heihe City, Heilongjiang Province, on the Amur River bordering with Russia. For over fifty years, he has done ethnological and cultural anthropological research and field work on Chinese peoples of the Altaic language family and the cultural heritage of shamanism as it has been passed down for generations among ethnic groups in northern China. He has dedicated his life to exploring, organizing, and translating ancient shamanic myths, rituals, divine oracles, taboos, spiritual healing methods, and the astronomy of the Manchu, Mongol, Oroqen, Evenki, Daur, Xibe, Hezhe, and other ethnic peoples, and his work has been widely recognized in the academic community and made him an influential leader in the study of Chinese shamanism. Fu Yuguang undertook two projects of the National Social Science Foundation and was in charge of shooting fifteen videos of the shamanic customs and traditions of Manchus living in Inner Mongolia and northeastern China. He has published important Manchu works and books and more than a hundred significant papers in journals at home and abroad, some of which have won awards. Although the author now has cerebral thrombosis, uses a wheelchair, and has become blind in one eye, he remains actively engaged in the study of ethnic peoples. He is currently a member of the Jilin Research Institute of Culture and History and the Provincial Intangible Cultural Heritage Expert Group, a researcher of the Jilin Provincial Center of Ethnic and Religious Studies, and an honorary director of the Shamanistic Research Institute of Changchun University.

Fu has received numerous honours and awards: in 2004, the Award for Scholarly Excellence of the International Society for Shamanistic Research; in 2007, the Chinese Folk Literature and Art *Shanhua* Award and the Folk Literature and Art Achievement Award; in 2008, the Changbaishan Literature and Art and Achievement Award of the Jilin provincial government; in 2009, the title of advanced individual safeguarding the intangible cultural heritage by the Ministry of Culture; and the title of inheritor of the Manchu *Shuobu* National Intangible Cultural Heritage. Since 1993, he has been granted a special government allowance from the State Council for his outstanding contributions to the social sciences.

Major publications:

Shamanism and Mythology (*Samanjiao yu shenhua*, 萨满教与神话), Liaoning University Press, 1990.

Study on Manchu Shamanism (*Manzu samanjiao yanjiu*, 满族萨满教研究), with Meng Huiying (孟慧英), Peking University Press, 1991.

Goddesses of Shamanism (*Samanjiao nvshen*, 萨满教女神), with Wang Honggang (王宏刚), Liaoning People's Publishing House, 1995.

Shaman (*Samanlu*, 萨满论), Liaoning People's Publishing House, 2000.

Fu Yuguang's Collected Works of Folk Culture (*Fuyuguang minsu wenhua lunji*, 富育光民俗文化论集), Jilin University Press, 2005.

Shamanic Culture (*Saman wenhualun*, 萨满文化论), with Guo Shuyun (郭淑云), Taiwan Student Book Company, 2005.

Shamanic Art (*Saman yishulun*, 萨满艺术论), Beijing Xueyuan Publishing House, 2009.

Investigations on the Cultural Heritages of Manchu Shamanism (*Manzu saman wenhua yicun diaocha*, 满族萨满文化遗存调查), with Zhao Zhizhong (赵志忠), Ethnic Publishing House Publishing House, 2010.

Notes on Shamanic Culture (*Manzu wenhua shouji*, 萨满文化手记), Beijing Xueyuan Publishing House, 2015.

Fu Yuguang's Collected Works (*Fu Yuguang wenji*, 富育光文集), vols I and II, Jilin People's Publishing House, 2017

Representative compilations:

Colorful Holy Fire: Selected Manchu Folktales (*Manzu minjian chuanshuoxuan qicai shenhuo*, 满族民间传说选<七彩神火>), Jilin People's Publishing House, 1984.

Legend of Kangxi (*Kangxi de chuanshuo*, 康熙的传说), with Wang Honggang (王宏刚), China Folk Literature and Art Publishing House, 1985.

Studies on Shamanic Culture (*Samanjiao wenhua yanjiu*, 萨满教文化研究), Vol. I, one of the chief editors, Jilin People's Publishing House, 1988.

Anecdotes of A Dissolute King (*Fengliu hanwang mizhuan*, 风流罕王秘传), with Yu Youyan (于又燕), China Federation of Literary and Art Circles Publishing House, 1989.

Dictionary of Religions and Myths of Ethnic Groups of China (*Zhongguo geminzu*) *zongjiao yu shenhua dacidian*, 中国各民族宗教与神话大辞典), chief Jilin editor, Xueyuan Publishing House, 1990.

Manchu Dictionary (*Manzu dacidian*, 满族大辞典), coauthor, Liaoning University Press, 1990.

Studies on Shamanic Culture (*Samanjiao wenhua yanjiu*, 萨满教文化研究), Vol. II, one of the chief editor Tianjin Ancient Books Publishing House, 1990.

Dictionary of Chinese Symbols (*Zhongguo xiangzheng cidian*, 中国象征辞典), coauthor, Tianjin Education Publishing House, 1991.

Manchu Social Life and Customs (*Manzu fengsuzhi*, 满族风俗志), with Wang Honggang (王宏刚), Minzu University of China Publishing House, 1991.

Encyclopedia of Jilin Province (*Jilinsheng baike quanshu*, 吉林省百科全书), vols I and II, author and associate editor, Jilin People's Publishing House, 1998.

Dictionary of Religion (*Zongjiao dacidian*, 宗教大辞典) coauthor, Shanghai Dictionary Publishing House, 1998.

Dictionary of Chinese Mythological Figures (*Zhongguo shenhua renwu dacidian* 中国神话人物辞典), coauthor, Shanxi People's Publishing House, 1998.

Collected Materials of Primordial Religions of Chinese Ethnic Groups (*Zhongguo geminzu yuanshi zongjiao ziliao jicheng*, 中国各民族原始宗教资料集成), author of Manchu Volume, China Social Sciences Press, 1999.

Chinese Folk Cultures (*Zhongguo minsu wenhua daguan*, 中国民俗文化大观), vols I and II, author and associate editor, Jilin People's Publishing House, 1999.

Living Shamans: Chinese Shamanism (*Huozhede saman-zhongguosamjiao*, 活着的萨满---中国萨满教), general consultor and coauthor, Liaoning People's Publishing House, 2001.

Pictures of Chinese Manchu Customs and Traditions (*Tuxiang zhongguo manzu fengsu xulu*图像中国满族风俗叙录), chief editor, Shandong Pictorial Publishing House, 2008.

Golden Mouth: Collected Manchu Traditional Storytelling (*Jinzi yiyang de zui-manzu chuantong shuobu wenji*, 金子一样的嘴-满族传统说部文集), chief editor, Xueyuan Publishing House, 2009.

Collected Manchu Shamanic Folk Works (Manzu minjian saman shenshu jicheng满族民间萨满神书集成), with Zhang Xuehui (张学慧), Jilin People's Publishing House, 2017.

Publications of traditional Manchu *Shuobu* (说部, storytelling):

The traditional Manchu *Shuobu*, which has been listed as a National Intangible Cultural Heritage by the State Council, has made significant contributions to the study of the Qing history and Chinese frontier and ethnic relations. The threefold series of *Shuobu* collected and organized by me and published by Jilin People's Publishing House consist of twenty-one volumes and six million Chinese characters.

First series, 2007:

Records of Grievances of the East Sea, vols I and II (*Donghai chenyuanlv*东海沉冤录); *Legend of General Sabusu*, vols I and II (*Sadaren zhuan*萨大人传) *Legends of Three Maidens*, vols I and II (*Feixiao sanqiao chuanqi*飞啸三巧传奇); *Heroic Mother and Son* (*Xuefei niangniang he baolugahan*

雪妃娘娘和包鲁嘎罕); *The Legend of Nishan Shaman*, vols I and II (*Nishan saman* 尼山萨满传); and annotated and organized six thousand lines of the East Sea shaman epic *Umesiben Mama* ("Wubuxiben mama" 乌布西奔妈妈).

Second series, 2009:

Enche Boucou (*Enqie buku* 恩切布库); *War in Heaven: Xilin Anban Mafa* (*Tiangong dazhan xilin'anbanmafa* 天宫大战: 西林安班玛发); and *Sumu Mama: Creation Myth and Tale* (*Sumu mama chuangshi shenhua yu chuanshuo* 苏木妈妈: 创世神话与传说).

Third series, 2016:

Legends of Nurhaci and Wanggao (*Liangshi hanwangzhuan · wanggao hanwangzhuan* 两世罕王传·王杲罕王传); *Master Boatmaker Sahaliyan* (*Sahalian chuanwang*萨哈连船王); *Legend of King Xueshan* (*Xueshan hanwanzhuan*雪山罕王传); *The Story of Likunzhu's Wedding Escape* (*Likunzhu tiaohunji*莉昆珠逃婚记); *Zhahutai Mama* (*Zhajutai mama*扎呼泰妈妈); *The Tribute of River Beluga* (*Huangyu gong*鳇鱼贡); and so on.

Liang Yanjun
Dalian, November 2019

Preface to the 1990 Chinese edition

The Chinese nation is a community of fifty-six ethnic nationalities, all of which have contributed to China as a whole from the bounty of their own cultural heritages. For a long time, however, we in China have not well understood the social history of some of these peoples. After the founding of the People's Republic of China, relevant ethnic policies were implemented, so this situation began to change.

In 1956, the Central Committee of the Communist Party of China launched a nationwide survey of the customs and languages of minority peoples, focusing on socioeconomic structures and modes of livelihood. Due to the limitations of those times, the means of investigation lacked modern electronic tools, and even photographic equipment was not always available. If we had the present equipment, the materials that were saved would be more complete. As for primordial religion, only a general survey was made, because there was little understanding of Indigenous religions and integral parts of the social life of this people. Nonetheless, we initiated a formidable undertaking that had never been done by our predecessors, seeking to understand the basic socioeconomic conditions of the fifty-six nationalities. We gathered basic data for the formulation of ethnic policies, the development of ethnic economies, and the training of the first batch of Chinese ethnological researchers who could pursue further investigations of the field. With the development of the national economy and the implementation of national policies, social science research in China has seen a remarkable development. The ancient classics and documents of the Yi and Naxi peoples of southwest China have been systematically collated and translated, as have classical Mongol and Tibetan texts; and the shamanist cultures of northeast China have begun to be systematically and thoroughly investigated. Now China is facing a great era of opening-up and development, and understanding the evolution of China's ethnic cultures would contribute to the world at large. For various reasons, research on the various ethnic cultures of China has been unbalanced, but our ethnological research is advancing.

I am now glad to welcome the publication of Fu Yuguang's book *Shamanism and Myth.* The author has engaged in research on northern shamanism for many years, and the book deserves praise as the first systematic investigation of shamanism in China. Research in the social sciences needs to be comprehensive, comparative, and integrated and based on precise and solid classifications. This book is a model of such research. It constitutes a living monument to the historical heritage of shamanism in the region. On the basis of the author's first-hand investigations, but with numerous references to ancient Chinese texts and foreign scholarly literature, the book opens up new horizons for ethnological and anthropological study. This new field of shamanic research needs to be pursued by aspiring young scholars, and I look forward to the field's flourishing as they follow in Fu Yuguang's footsteps.

Ren Jiyu
September 1990
Beijing

Introduction to the English edition

It is an honour for me to write the introduction of this valuable book. For more than forty years, noted scholar Fu Yuguang has dedicated himself to rescuing and studying the shamanic legacy that has been passed down among his native Manchu and other Altaic peoples of northern China. He has done so in the footsteps of his father, Fu Xilu (富希陆), who began gathering folk materials while teaching in Aihui County on the banks of the Amur in the 1930s, when Fu was born. Fu Yuguang's own research is not just a matter of pouring over old documents at a scholarly distance. As he is happy to say, he lived for years in ethnic villages, eating, working, singing, and dancing with the local people; forming lasting friendships; and learning to sing the sacred chants, make spirit idols, and beat the drum in shamanic rituals. The present book, originally titled *Shamanism and Mythology*, is valuable not just because of its rich panorama of the rites, myths, and shamanic lore of the Manchu, Mongol, and other northern peoples but also because of the local colour and immediacy that his first-hand experiences bring to the material and for his insightful perspective on northern shamans' social, cultural, and religious roles.

Fu tells of entranced shamans inspired by the gods and is well aware of the mythic hero Nisan Shaman, who can travel to the underworld to retrieve dead souls. But for him, a northern shaman is not in the Eliade mould of one who makes ecstatic journeys to the otherworld. Rather, they stand out as one who has extraordinary sensitivity to the everyday needs of the common people and who can use that power to be of down-to-earth, practical service. The author seeks to break out of what he sees as the scholarly fixation on shamanic "spirituality" and trance contact with spirit worlds and recover an appreciation of shamans' original function as clan sages, the embodiments of the clan's spirit, wisdom, and power. They are respected as being well versed in clan history and adept at healing, sacrificial procedures, and the use of traditional chants and dances to ease peoples' anxieties and draw them out of their everyday perceptions of reality into a common mystic realm. Shamans deal with a plethora of nature and ancestral spirits, but their spiritual achievements do not have their origin only in so-called divine powers. Fu quotes an elderly shaman who once said that "In ancient times, divinity indicated limitless scope. You become godlike if you understand people's thinking, longing, imaginings and expectations."

Some of Fulim Yuguang's research has been translated and introduced to scholars abroad, but we are now fortunate to have in English his 1990 first work, translated under the title *Shamanic and Mythic Cultures of Ethnic Peoples in Northern China*.

In its present layout, the first volume begins with discussions of the spirit world of northern shamanism. The author points out that "shaman," *saman* (萨满), is a Jurchen word with the root meaning of "knowing" and stresses that the shaman is the embodiment of their "clan's spirit, wisdom, and power." The original religion of northern peoples, shamanism is an evolving religious belief that is based on the idea that deities and spirits are everywhere, but it is rooted in specific conditions of the freezing north. Northern shamanism worships the sun for its life-giving role, along with certain animals of the northern wilds. From a theoretical point of view, it focuses on manifestations of spirit energy (*qi*气), the notion that human beings have three souls, and the ancient idea of multiple heavens. Fu maintains that exploring the ideology of northern ethnic cultures requires looking at concrete aspects of the Indigenous culture and history, not just generic trends of thought.

In line with this view, Chapter 2 discusses the worship of nature deities, often female: sun, moon, stars, mother earth, fire, water, magpies, crows, and local waterfowl. In Chapter 3, Fu introduces the worship of ancestors and fertility goddesses, noting that the dominant Manchu male god of heaven, Abka Enduri, was initially the female deity Abka Hehe.

The next three chapters cover rituals, beginning in Chapter 4 with what Fu regards as the most ancient shamanic ritual, blood sacrifice. He sees this is being in line with the life-giving power of blood and perhaps the notions that blood serves as a medium for floating souls as they wander about outside the body. Fu also gives lively descriptions of Mongol and Manchu rites that worship fire for its power for cleansing and casting off the cold of northern winters. In Chapter 5, he gives detailed descriptions of rites worshipping the stars. As ancient peoples began to settle down, they formulated laws concerning the positions and alterations the stars, which Fu summarizes in a mythical/astronomical chart. He also describes rites worshipping the East Sea and those worshipping willows as indicators of a nearby water fountainhead and so symbols of life. Chapter 6 presents enlightening discussions of the *tangse* shine rites of the Qing court against the background of the portable *tangse* shines used by ordinary Manchu when migrating. Then discussions of Manchu *jia* folk rituals as they came to be formalized in line with Qing norms follow.

In the second volume, Chapter 1 focuses on divination, which clan records and Fu's own observations show to be intricately bound up with northern shaman activities. The author understands divination as being based on the belief that everything has a soul and stresses that divining is indispensable when choosing new shamans. He traces the documented history of divination in China, going back almost three thousand years, and then analyses specific forms of northern shamanic divination, in particular the reading of bones and interpretation of dreams.

The following chapters deal with myths. Chapter 2 gives valuable background information concerning the shamanic roots of northern myths, noting that shamans have continually added new episodes to traditional mythic tales. Fu discusses the interrelationship of the myths of Tungus peoples and the infiltration of Han motifs in their mythic tradition in the form of tales of the underworld and ghosts. He describes methods of mythic transmission, such as the clan chant contests that go back to Jurchen times. He then gives examples of myths focused on the goddesses and animals involved in creation, enlivening the material with quotes from mythic chants. Chapter 3 invites us to sample the whole array of narrative segments from the Manchu creation myth "War in Heaven." Chapter 4 introduces individual tribal myths and burial customs, rounding out the earlier discussion on ancestor worship.

In Chapter 5, the author gives a lengthy treatise on spirit idols, suggesting that they may have come about with the rise of ancestor worship and belief in souls. Although they originally involved animistic worship, Fu maintains that they became what can truly be called idol worship only once they began to take on human or half-human features. He goes on to give intriguing accounts of how particular idols came to be revealed in dreams and ritual trance sessions and then fashioned accordingly. Since the ability of ancestral idols to protect the tribe depends on the power of their eyes, people have to give great care to fashioning the eyes. Since idols have great thirst for the life-giving power of blood, they need then to periodically offer the idols fresh blood in sacrificial rituals.

Chapter 6 ends the book with typical traits of northern shamans, first as depicted in Indigenous myths, for which he uses quotes from the Jurchen shamanic epic *Umesiben Mama*, and then as understood by modern scholars. Fu states the idea that underlies his research as a whole: northern Chinese shamans do not fit into Eliade's model of people caught up in ecstatic journeys to supernatural worlds; rather, they are respected by their clans for their unusually keen human powers of sensitive perception and their efforts to hone these powers to aid clan members in everyday situations.

Daniel Kister
Seoul, October 2019

Introduction

Like many aspects of the ethnic cultures of northern China, shamanism arouses enthusiastic interest and wonder throughout the whole world. From the viewpoint of history, it can be considered the mother of all ethnic cultures, and the personality and the psychology of northern peoples have been shaped from generation to generation by numerous shamanic factors, including shaman dress, the beat of the shaman's drum, hawk and tiger dances, age-old myths and heroic epics, ancient secret histories, old precepts, secret divination practices known only to shamans, and the medicinal use of herbs, along with extensive ancestral experience in harnessing fire, flood control, catching fish and birds, nursing babies, training in cosmic teachings, the identification of stars, warfare drills, and other skills. In a threefold role of master, deity, and soul, a shaman inherits the spiritual heritage of their ethnic group. In the past, the influence of shamanism was felt in all households in the vast areas of the Changbai Mountains and Heilong River (Amur); and it has left its traces throughout North and Northeast Asia. As many domestic and foreign scholars noticed early on, shamanism has not faded out among the northern Chinese peoples or come to have less influence on them over the passing of time. Many scholars have lived in the rough with peasants to both research and appreciate the mystic aspects of these northern ethnic cultures and uncover the mysteries of the religious beliefs common in this part of the world.

I had a joyful experience in the course of the spring snows of 1990 while deep in the Greater Khingan Range in Heilongjiang Province. The aged Oroqen shaman Meng Jinfu (孟金福) was invited to perform songs and dances for us to the same beat of the drum used when hunting elk. At a young age, Meng was taught his musical skills by a spirit, and in accord with his forceful beat, all present clapped their hands to the music – an exciting event indeed. After the April Grain Rain Days (Guyu谷雨), one of the twenty-four solar seasonal terms marking the season when abundant rainfall is needed for sowing crops, we discovered a Manchu family's shamanic treasures that had been well preserved for over several hundred years. There were manuscripts of inspired shamanic utterances, spirit statuettes, figurines, and other objects dating back more than two hundred years, and we found that of all recently discovered artefacts from the Qing era, these are the oldest ones depicting nature worship and ancestor worship. They thus have great worth as both research objects and historic art finds.

The word "shaman" is written in different ways in Chinese: *shaman* (沙曼), *sama* (萨玛), *shama* (沙玛), *sama* (撒麻), *saman* (撒瞒), *shanman* (珊蛮), and so on. The earliest written mention of the term occurs in *Documents of the Three Reigns' Northern Alliance* (*Sanchao Beimeng Huibian*) compiled by Xu Mengshen (徐梦莘) of Southern Song (1127 – 1279). It is said there that "*shanman*" is a Jurchen term for a sorcerer who has divine power. Since the Jin (1115–1234) and Yuan (1279–1368) dynasties, various terms have been used, but now *saman* is in common Chinese usage. It is, in fact, a Jurchen word, the Jurchen language belonging to a Manchu branch of the Altaic language family. The term is often explained as *wu* (巫). In Chinese, following Ling Chunsheng, who defined it in this way, scholars of different countries define what a shaman is differently, on the basis of the external characteristics of their shamans. A shaman is often described as a person afflicted with some sort of mania, some national encyclopaedias defining "shaman" as "madman" or "a person who has mania." In Soviet Russia, some scholars have defined the person as "one who loses control upon onset of the disease," and others argue that a shaman is not "a normal person" but rather "a maniac."

Despite these various proposals, such definitions and descriptions do not make the term "shaman" clear. We can, however, also look for meaning from its etymological roots. In the Manchu, Hezhe, Xibe, and Oroqen languages, the root "*sa*" or "*za*" means "to know," and "to know" is pronounced "*sam*" or "*zam*." In Manchu and Hezhe, the sound "*sam*" means "to know" and "*saha*" means "to have known it." Thus, "to know" is what *saman* essentially means. In the well-known Manchu shaman epic *Umesiben Mama*, a shaman is "a person who knows all" (*ha juseen*). A shaman knows best what the spirits mean to communicate to us and serves as a bond with the spirits, and all that the shaman does is blessed by the spirits. A shaman thus enjoys great respect among the masses. In later Manchu oracles, in line with the meaning of *ha juseen* as a person who knows all things, shamans were venerated as "*abka juse*" or "*aha juse*," suggesting that they are intermediaries between spirits and human beings. A shaman's functions and abilities are clearly defined.

Regarding a shaman as mentally ill amounts to a completely flawed appreciation of the origin and characteristics of shamanic activity. In fact, none of the shamans of northern China or famous shamans of the past is mentally ill. On the contrary, they are by definition the wise people of each ethnic group. In some Manchu clans, a shaman is said to "have a golden tongue and great courage and wisdom." To a certain extent, a shaman is an embodiment of the clan's spirit, wisdom, and power. In daily life, shamans are simply clan members and enjoy no special privileges, but they will fearlessly rush in when an individual clansperson or the clan as a whole is in danger. Shamans serve as native doctors and guardians, shouldering the responsibility for the development and prosperity of the clan. It is said that without a shaman, a clan "cannot shine forever like the sun." The reverence shown to shamans derives from many factors, including the rules for selecting a shaman, which have a close connection with shamanic concepts of primitive psychology, such as spirit transformation and the expenditure of vital energy (*qi* 气).

Shamanism is the original religion of northern Chinese peoples. As Cao Yanjie stated in *Records of Eastern Siberia* (*Xiboliyadongpian jiyao*), shamanic "trance dance and folk customs have spread wide from the three rivers – Sungari, Amur, and Ussuri – the northeastern estuary" (Cao Yanjie 1934). As an Indigenous religion, shamanism is an inherited, closed tradition rigorously transmitted within the clan. Some foreign travel books before the Qing dynasty speak of it, and Qing dynasty records, notes, and historical texts of northern China present brief accounts of shamanic activity. Formal investigations and detailed observations of northern shamanic cultures did not begin until the early period of the Republic of China (1912–1949). At that time, Ling Chunsheng initiated field surveys of shamanic rites and customs. In line with his own field visits and the artefacts he observed, he made comparative analyses and wrote the classic work *The Goldi Tribe on the Lower Sungari River* (*Songhuajiang xiayou de hezhezu*). Published in 1934, the work brought him high prestige in China and beyond for its wealth of shamanic lore. Other Chinese scholars of that period discussed the concept and influence of shamanism or the shaman on the northern peoples in their articles as well.

Nevertheless, shamanism began to be systematically studied in China only after the 1950s. Shaman folk beliefs and customs were not distinguished form witchcraft and superstition at the time of the founding of the People's Republic of China in 1949, and this delayed saving shamanic culture. In the 1950s, scholars of ethnology, history, and economics initiated massive sociohistorical investigations on all Chinese ethnic areas under the competitive authorities according to state ethnic policy. These first investigations surveyed in the northeast region of China helped bring together a large team of ethnologists and blazed a trail with new methods for studying shamanic culture. Northern peoples praised them highly for their great efforts, and their hard work gave rise to a new academic subject: northern ethnology.

Chinese studies on the northern region progressed materially and intellectually, and after the Reform and Opening-up of the late 1980s,[1] ethnic studies came into their heyday. The cultural heritage of the region, including shamanic culture, was gradually rescued from oblivion with the collecting, translating, and editing of numerous materials. Many valuable books could appear in print, and since then, many well-preserved manuscripts and ethnic artefacts of the Manchu, Daur, Oroqen, Ewenki, Mongol, Xibe, and Hezhe that had been treasured for centuries have been collected. Now, prestigious shamans, singers, storytellers, and folk artisans are given their due respect. Although these reform-oriented investigations set the scene for future cultural research, researchers did not know enough about Indigenous beliefs, folk customs, or oral literature or in particular about Manchu culture. The ten years of turmoil from 1966 to 1976[2] did away with many inheritors of the tradition and rare materials. That tragedy has left many gaps to be filled, and despite scholars' great efforts over the years, there are still many unresolved questions due to the shortage of primary sources. If we are now too slow in saving what we have left of shamanic culture, the history of northern ethnic peoples will never be uncovered, let alone truly understood.

I have a deep love for shamanic culture, and I hold a strong belief that no ambiguity or imprecision should be allowed in academic research and history.

Shamanic culture varies greatly with its long history, making it difficult for us to lay bare its true nature. How large is the cultural circle of shamanism? How can we truly understand its influence on China? What value and meaning does it hold in China? Some Chinese and foreign scholars argue that all original religious traditions can be categorized as shamanic. This concept, however, tries to include too much. As a primitive form of religious culture that prevailed in a sub-frigid zone and a northern frigid zone across Northern Europe, North Asia, and North America, the cultural circle of shamanism reflects strong localized tendencies of the isolated living habits of Indigenous peoples over time. The precise differences between shamanism and witchcraft or sorcery has confounded scholars for a long while. What are the differences and similarities? Japan's politically oriented investigations in Manchuria (the old name for the Manchu nationality or northeastern China) in the early 1930s combined and conflated ethnic shamanism with sheer superstition and shamans with cheats who extort money for prayers or even with murderers, and nowadays, shamanic rituals are spoken of as "evil spirit dances" (*tiaodashen*, 跳大神). We can take two approaches to shamanic activity: we can regard all shamanic practices as "pure superstition" and try only to prevent them from doing harm, or we can discard the dross and retain the essence for beneficial use. We need to understand shamanism as a primitive religion born at the dawn of human civilization that inevitably has had bright and dark aspects over the course of time, but we must come to realize that it constitutes a treasure trove of cultural wisdom and a rich spiritual legacy.

From a more international perspective, the cultural circle of shamanism is located in the temperate zone, sub-frigid zone, and frigid zone of the northern hemisphere. Foreign investigations into shamanism date back more than two hundred years. In the eyes of Westerners, shamanism has been seen as a key to uncovering mysteries of human history and culture and as a cultural repository in its own right. So they have shown great interest in it, founding academic institutions and publishing journals and monographs. At the same time, shamantology took shape as a healing and meditation movement and continues to this day. As a rare cultural heritage for the modern world, shamanism preserves what humankind learned and felt in the hard times when the ancients explored and conquered nature. It is a "living fossil" of original modes of human thought and civilization.

As far as China is concerned, it is the home country of shamanism, and it has kept intact many ethnic treasures of shamanic culture for thousands of years. Research on Chinese shamanism has thus come into worldwide notice as a vital part of the international shamanic community. The sociohistorical conditions of northeast China have made it possible to preserve shamanism intact. In the three northeastern provinces of Liaoning, Jilin, and Heilongjiang, the Manchu, Oroqen, Daur, and Ewenki not only accept it as their spiritual legacy but also perform living shamanic activities, and such performances serve as signs of its overwhelming influence. Some families in the area have preserved inspired shamanic utterances transcripts, sacrificial artefacts, and ritual costumes dating from the foundation of the Later Jin dynasty, specifically in 1616. Primitive nature rites have never been interrupted, including sea sacrifice, fire sacrifice, and the ancient Manchu *ye* ritual

(*Yeji*, 野祭) held to worship mountains, rivers, stars, the sun and the moon, and all living creatures while inculcating love and respect for nature. From the perspective of global cultural ideology, the original star maps, ancient medicinal lore, and divination techniques that have been handed down are crucial. In Xinjiang, too, the Xibe people in Qapqal Autonomous County still keep rare shamanic scripts and ritual tales, and in eastern Inner Mongolia, the Mongols have inherited shamanic beliefs and maintain the activity of their *boo* (shaman) as a distinct form of religion different from Tibetan Buddhism.

Primordial religious beliefs developed from primitive ideologies rooted in specific regional conditions. By analysing shamanist beliefs and practices, we can understand northern ancestors' primitive ideology and explore the origin of human civilization in the region. Humanity's childhood is a wonder and a mystery. Ethnic and national boundaries appeared later, as history evolved, but the concept of religion appeared far earlier than that of nation, and fledgling religious worship was never limited to any specific ethnicity or nation.

This book seeks first and foremost to explore the common ideology underlying the birth of northern ethnic cultures. To do so, we need to look into concrete aspects of pre-ethnic culture and history, not just generic trends of knowledge. It is only in this way that we can understand the lineage of ethnic culture and cement the cohesion of national unity and promote the flourishing of our many Indigenous cultures. Second, along this path of research, the book focuses on the shamanic cultures in Siberia and Far East Asia, aiming to get a clear picture of the unique traits of northern shamanism. Third, the book enthusiastically presents the field survey materials accumulated over decades. For reliability and research integrity and to authenticate the references and correctly annotate the folktales cited, I visited shamans, clan chiefs, and singers from northeast China.

In recent years, many forward-looking scholars in China have begun to understand and emphasize the importance of northern shamanic cultures. They have developed a strong interest in shamanist research and begun to redefine it as a cross-disciplinary field of study that demands due consideration in history, aesthetics, sociology, cultural anthropology, religion, folklore, and archaeology. All these various disciplines serve not only to absorb rich research nutrients from the shamanic culture but also to open up new ways of proceeding in existing fields of research. Of course, this is an international subject. I am confident that all scholars in China and beyond will join hands to uncover the mysteries of shamanism, even though it is a tortuous journey.

Notes

1 Here and elsewhere in this book, some quotations of foreign authors are from a Chinese translation and so not identical to the author's original words. In some cases, the page or other reference for cited materials is lacking in the original Chinese book and cannot easily be located. Reform and Opening-up were part of a policy of opening up to the outside world implemented by the Chinese government in 1978.

2 The ten years of turmoil refer to the Great Proletarian Cultural Revolution that took place during those years.

1 The spirit world of northern shamanism

1.1 The operational laws of the spirits

The essential concept of shamanism in any region or ethnic group is the following: All beings in the cosmos that human beings depend on, living and nonliving, constitute an abode of deities and spirits who are present everywhere, give rise to everything, and possess everything. This is why they are so earnestly worshipped. This pantheistic conception constitutes the basis for an understanding of shaman deities and spirits and the ground on which shamanic perceptions and modes of expression in all sacrificial rituals in northern China is rooted.

To study shaman spirits, we must first know what spirit activity means in northern Chinese shamanism. Every ethnic group in northern China has its spirit-chosen shaman, who acts as an intermediary between human beings and spirits and serves as the spirits' representative and mouthpiece. Shamans state unequivocally that gods and spirits really exist. They are celestial beings, and they have almighty power. A spiritual being is a substance made up of *qi* (气: literally "breath," "air," or "gas"; figuratively "material energy"), an invisible force that people know but cannot see, the active principle of any living thing. In most cases in shamanic belief, however, a spirit exerts their power and influence through a physical substance. A shaman who attains a supernatural level will state not only that supernatural power exists but also that they can feel that power. It possesses a shaman's body, coming suddenly and going quickly. That power may influence the shaman's own vital energy and may even command a shaman in trance to act supernaturally or ecstatically. In shamanic parlance, such phenomena are referred to as the coming of the spirit, presence of the spirit, or possession by the spirit. Only a person who can experience this is a true shaman, a proper medium between the spirits and human beings. Only such a shaman can communicate with spirits and keenly observe how they behave. A shaman who reaches this level can hear, see, perceive, know, and understand all phenomena in the supernatural world. Moreover, they can discover the dwellings of cosmic spirits at any time and communicate with them. In a word, a true shaman can move freely between the spiritual world and the earthly world. According to veteran Chinese shamans, this is the way to thoroughly understand the basic operational laws of the spirits.

What does the operational laws of the spirits mean? It goes beyond the understanding of common people. It points to supernatural power beyond the human that embraces all beings in the cosmos. It is, in fact, a primitive form of pantheism. In the minds of ancient peoples, everything around them, supernatural or wondrous, was a life-threatening danger. The psychological mechanism behind their worship amounted to trying to counteract or defend themselves against such danger. In northern China, this led them to believe in a wide variety of types of spirits. According to shamanic beliefs of northern peoples, there are various spiritual beings in the universe, each with their own ideas, likings, habits, endowments, tastes, and personalities, which are not subject to interference from the earthly world. They live and move in accord with their own primordial principles of generation and their respective orbits of activity.

Spirits act independently in their worlds, which are separate from ours. In the northern Chinese understanding of shamanic gods and spirits, they have urges, emotions, ideas, and character traits like us on the one hand; on the other, they possess amazing power, which can be categorized according to various criteria, such as locality, nature, status, size, level of ability, distance, and good or evil. They descend to mortal beings or communicate with them by the channels of prayer, sacrificial rituals, and dreams, and they may use or possess a medium to bring about the object of their prayers once the prayers have been conveyed to them. Only a shaman assigned by a particular spirit can feel, see, hear, and understand that spirit's presence and wishes. This is because only the shaman can sense the primordial operational laws of the spirits. If people want to know or invite a spirit, shamans need to enter the spirit realm through ritual.

Each deity and each spirit have their own origin, such as materially embodied spirits, human spirits, animal spirits, and nature spirits. Every natural phenomena, such as thunder and lightning, rivers and lakes, and the sun and the moon, may have a supernatural power and so can be called god or spirit, in both cases in Chinese *shen* (神). The world that they inhabit can be shown as follows:

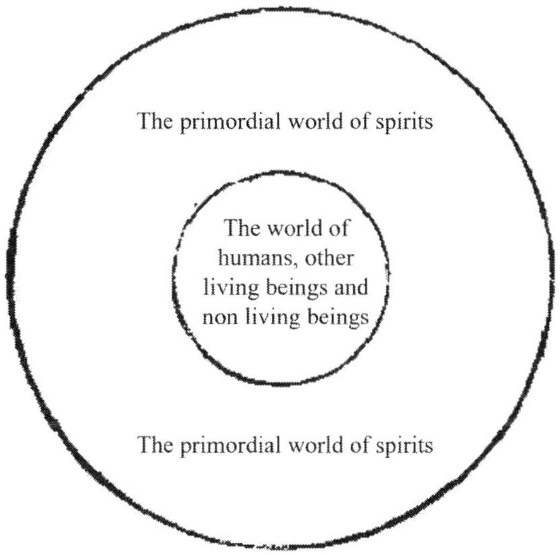

The diagram shows that beyond the mortal world, there are cosmic spaces or a divine world in which spirit beings live and from which they can travel to the world of the inner circle as they like. All this constitutes the primordial pantheistic world of northern Chinese shamanism. The ideas and beliefs associated with it have risen from specific sociohistorical conditions bound up with people's means of livelihood and mindset. Over the long history of the shamanic pantheism in China, its meaning has varied greatly.

1.2 The evolution of northern shamanism

Religious reflections on the fragility of human beings in our fight for survival against nature, no doubt, did not come with the first origins of humankind. Archaeology has confirmed that in the era when primitive groups of human beings separated themselves from animals, their thinking was underdeveloped. At that time, it can hardly be thought that they could form religious concepts or perform acts of worship, because they probably could not distinguish themselves from the natural world to which they had adapted. Ancient religion must have surfaced in primitive tribal society only after their mode of thinking became further developed. That Neanderthals of the mid-Palaeolithic period had a budding form of religious worship is attested to by archaeological findings that they had acquired customs, such as when burying the dead, they placed ram horns around the body and scattered chips of red stone around the remains.

As for northern China, definitive relics of budding shamanism have been rarely discerned, analysed, or identified, and it is difficult to date their earliest appearance. Red hematite powder, however, was sprinkled around the bone fossils in the Upper Cave in Zhoukoudian, Beijing, from the late Palaeolithic period, and flint stones, teeth with drilled holes, cockle shells, bone pendants, and other burial objects were scattered around the corpses, along with the sprinkled powder. All this indicates that the cavepeople there had come to have primitive religious notions about eighteen thousand years ago. According to local folk belief in northern China, red powder, standing for blood, reflects people's desire to soothe the souls of the deceased. Archaeological investigations have disclosed that in northeast China and in Siberia, many remains and skeletons dating back to the Palaeolithic period and the Neolithic period were buried amid similar objects. At Siunvge, northeast of Moscow, the remains of an adult male and a boy were similarly sprinkled with red ochre powder and those of the adult with three thousand beads, animal teeth, mammoth tusks, and other ornaments. Examples of other artefacts unearthed in China are the bone-carved hawk's head; fish and pottery figurines; and patterns of a dog, a pig, a bear, and water ripples, all on shards from Xinkailiu in Jixi, Heilongjiang. In Yinggeling in Heilongjiang were grey pottery shaped in the form of birds, deer, sheep, and frogs, and there are primitive drawings on earthenware from Heilongjiang sites in Ang'angxi, Bai Jinbao and Qinghua. At Baicheng, the capital of the Jin dynasty (1115–1234) near the Ashi River, Heilongjiang, B.R. Tolmachevo unearthed a bronze vessel with two little birds carved in relief, which reflects the ancient worship of divine birds. All these totemic objects represent creatures worshipped in the periods of gathering and both fishing and hunting economies. They are the product of peoples who worshipped primordial shamanistic deities, and they show that clan societies of those times worshipped animals such as the eagle, fish, swine, bears, and deer.

For his part, Alexander Okladnikov, in *Archeological Discoveries in the Far East of the Soviet Union*, depicts in detail the cave paintings at Sakaci Aliyang left by the Jurchen ancestors of the Manchu before they moved to northern China. One of the paintings, as shown next, reflects their sun worship:

These petroglyphs reflect a Jurchen myth that has been passed down to this day, which begins as follows:

> Long, long ago, our earth was once all flooded, but some divine birds carried sand and stones to pile up a small patch of land on which human beings lived and multiplied. Blessed by the sun goddess, they thus had a chance to survive the flood, and all beings revived again.

The paintings point to the religious ideology and mythic concepts of the inhabitants of northern China and Northeast Asia in the distant past. They indicate that they brought their conceptual religious beliefs to life by countless physical artistic objects around the time of the transition from the Palaeolithic period to the Neolithic period. These old beliefs formed the soil for cultures in which shamanic ideology originated.

Along with the development of material means of production, the pantheistic ideology of shamanism was unceasingly enriched, improved as it evolved. In light of cultural artefacts available, its evolution falls into the following stages: The recently excavated Goddess Temple at Niuheliang Village, Liaoning, shows that there was a fully developed ideology of religious worship in northern China at least five thousand years ago. However, religious practices may well have extended back to more than a million years ago, and ancient relics verify the early birth of such activity in the region. Numerous artefacts have been unearthed that indicate that it began before clan-centred societies evolved. As human beings became homo sapiens, they, no doubt, sought to explain the cause of their fears and ease them. With their high intelligence quotient, humans adapted to life in their ever-changing natural environment, reproduced, and found means to extend their lifespan, and their environment drew them to think, explore, and seek out the power and means to conquer it. In this way, low-level beginnings of religious awe, worship, and prayer emerged.

This is evidenced by the ancient stone vessels unearthed in northern China that scholars understand as having religious significance. Some have a willow-leaf shape that resembles the female vulva: a symbol of human life and reproduction. Others are engraved with various other patterns, such as the following Palaeolithic figures that also exist as fish-scale patterns on modern shamans' costumes. They are taken from pendants on the ritual costumes and headdresses of Manchu shamans Lang (郎) and Xu (徐) that have been passed down for generations as heirlooms.

The first pattern might symbolize murky night, the second sunshine, the third rippling water or rising vapour, and the fourth heaven and earth. The figures, moreover, show that the thinking of human beings even in that ancient era was complex enough to express natural phenomena in abstract terms.

The most prominent aspect of shamanism is the worship of the cosmos, and that religious outlook apparently appeared early in the north as our pioneering ancestors sought to conquer nature in that chilly land. Sunshine and warmth are the first conditions for survival, so it is perhaps for this reason that the above patterns can be found on ancient stone tools in the region. We should not regard them as either chance scribbling or mimetic reflections of natural phenomena or simply aesthetic objects. They express what the ancients thought about life, their desires for light and warmth, their religious perceptions, their myths, their knowledge of the cycles of day and night, and their understanding of nature. They felt warm on the land and cold underground in summer and vice versa in winter. They wondered about natural phenomena and sought the forces behind them, and when they received no support from nature, they turned to the spiritual world for comfort. In great fear and awe, they thus worshipped all natural things, which they knew could protect them but could destroy them instead. They had no choice but to prayerfully entreat the forces of nature when they confronted them in their weakness and helplessness. These were the earliest ideas of shamanism of which we can find evidence. There is no evidence of religious rites based on a definite image of a deity.

Ever since its inception, however, shamanism has been advancing in its religious thinking along with evolving human society. From about forty thousand to ten thousand years ago, between the mid to late Palaeolithic period and early

(一) (二) (三) (四)

Neolithic period, our northern ancients entered into primordial clan society. The numerous manuscripts of ancient shamanic tales that have been collected are a rare cornucopia from which I infer that shamanism in the matriarchal era had by then matured with diversified characteristics and full-blown sacrificial rituals that would continue to develop as it then stepped into a more mature and more active phase in emerging clan society. Nature worship, totem worship, animism, and ideas of the soul all became imbedded in clan life and customs. The frequent celebration of colourful sacred sacrificial rites and reliance on judgements of the spirits in the form of oracles, spirit testing, and divination became typical of ancestral northern fishing and hunting peoples and took on strong regional features.

According to historical documents, next come the shamanistic developments of the Tungusic Sushen (Sušen) peoples: Jurchen (Nvzhen), Shiwei, Wuji, Mohe, Bohai, and others who lived in caves and trees in the north of China – fishing, farming, and using flint-headed arrows to hunt up into the Liao and Jin dynasties. With the Sushen, northern shamanism evolved from a matriarchal clan religion into a patriarchal one. The most important change in shamanic belief was that the worship of patriarchal ancestors and relevant sacrificial rites came to occupy a central position with earlier nature and animal worship. At the same time, the myriad deities and regulations and customs surrounding the rites became increasingly more complicated with the absorption of Buddhist, Taoist, and Confucian creeds and Han ritual practices, such that the original face of shamanism was greatly changed. Then, too, as endless migrations occurred, when some northern ethnic groups moved year after year, and some peoples were reunited after division and others divided after unification. Shamanism became a huge stream of multiple cultural currents, such that it is now exceedingly hard to trace it back to its original roots. Much research needs to be done to do so, and much has been done in recent years in both China and abroad in the way of identification, analysis, and sifting out data from primary sources. However, all this has actually added to the difficulty of probing the basic nature and significance of northern shamanism. Mistakes have been made in trying to do so, with shamanism's sometimes being almost equated with ordinary witchcraft.

Finally, from late Qing dynasty until the present, shamanism in northern China has been increasingly on the decline. In the early Qing dynasty (1644–1911), its Manchu founders incorporated their traditional shamanic beliefs and sacrificial rites into the Han palace rituals of previous dynasties. Descendants of the Jurchen, they held traditional Jurchen *tangse* rites (堂子祭) at the Qing imperial ritual shrine. In the seventeenth year of the reign of Qianlong, the sixth Qing emperor,[1] there was promulgated the *Manchu Trance Rites for the Worship of Heaven* (*Manzu tiaoshen jitian dianli*), which unified the entire system of shamanic rituals throughout the empire, completing the standardization and reformation of the traditional clan religion that had been going on for centuries in the north. From then on, shamanic rituals became simply a set of household ancestor rites. Some Manchu *hala* (clan in the Manchu language) and other ethnic groups, such as the Oroqen,[2] Daur,[3] Ewenki,[4] and Hezhe,[5] still keep alive the ancient rites – but with changes, due to the influence of Manchu royal rites and other factors. Since the Republic Period (1912–1949), moreover, the shaman rites have been held on a shrinking scale. As a primitive religion, northern shamanism has its original roots in the economic and cultural modes of life of ancient northern peoples, so it must necessarily downsize and wane with advances in civilization. In New China (since 1949), shaman rites and clan shamans have fallen into oblivion as elderly people die. It is now considered just a living fossil of history that attracts attention as ethnic cultural heritage.

1.3 Shamanic spirits

What is deity, in Chinese *shen* (神)? This has always been a main question for theology, religious studies and sociology. Each discipline focuses on different aspects, but they have one point in common: A deity is an invisible, unknowable, mysterious supernatural power. Alternatively, we might say that what is unknowable is deity or what is unpredictable in its *yin-yang*[6] is deity. Deity gives birth to all things. There is nothing stronger than thunder in driving all things, nothing faster than wind in moving them, nothing hotter than fire in drying them, nothing happier than lakes in nurturing them, nothing better than water in nourishing them, nothing more powerful than mountains in providing their beginning or end. Thus, water and fire attract each other and wind and thunder complement each other. Mountains and lakes communicate with each other. Thus come about all changes, which produces all things. Commentaries on the *Book of Changes* interpret "deity" as the result of five elements or phases that produce and complement one another. The central idea is that deity is the first cause of all movements, but it is too subtle to be seen or felt. Buddhism considers deity as unfathomable karma or an invisible superpower that affects the future. Taoism argues that what has magical power is a deity. All such power is the magic of a god or spirit. All these thoughts envelop the notion of deity with a sense of profound mystery. As is said of Confucius, however, in chapter VII of the *Analects* (*Lunyu*), "The subjects on which the Master did not talk were extraordinary things, feats of strength, disorder, and spiritual beings."

Primordial shamanism is a natural religion from humanity's childhood. It has no profound theoretical belief. From the words of master shamans as expressed by shamans in Manchu oracles and teachings, shamanist ideas of *shen* can mean deity, a deity, a spirit, spirits, supernatural, and mind – sometimes abstruse and fantastic yet realistic and sometimes simply materialistic. The veteran shaman of the Manchu Wu Hala (clan) Wu Botong said that *shen* is the mother of all things, but the author wants to say that it is the mind. It is what one perceives, senses, thinks, and hopes. It owns everything and exists everywhere. In a *jao'uyun* (traditional training class for Manchu shaman initiates), an old shaman of the Zang Hala (clan) taught shaman initiates that if one wants to really command shamanic techniques, one should not search out any magic or superpower but summon all the energies, powers, and forces of nature to serve onself. One has to practice again and again until one masters them. Then, a true divine being will come about – the "presence of the spirit." Yesong, the famous megashaman and chief of the Fuca Hala of Siji Village, Heilongjiang, once told shamans that

> Shen is power. It is not outside, but inside; not on the skin, but in the heart. Where your heart is, there is true *shen*; otherwise the divine presence disappears. Indeed, deity/spirit is everywhere, and it can summon all magical powers for its use. A shaman must be busy as a bee or ant, coming to really know the medicinal property of all herbs, the basic nature of all beasts, the flying nature of all birds, the dynamic nature of mountains, rivers, stars and the moon. If you don't know, don't understand, don't act, or are incapable, you're not a shaman!

Kvgvturi the great flying shaman and chief of the Manchu Qian Hala, once said,

> When I was nine years old, I dreamed of a pair of white eagles falling onto my chest. The tribesmen did not like them, so they built a fire to burn them to ashes. Seeing this, I dashed into the raging flames and suddenly jumped above the trees. I did not fall or have fear. That's *shen*! It is an act of gathering all one's powers together for one's self-use! Then I practiced *qinggong* (轻功, the prowess to fly). It's easy to jump over a tree canopy or mountain stream. Finally, I became a divine flying shaman.

Focusing on a different aspect of *shen*, Yu Kun, a megashaman of the Hu Hala said,

> All things have their *hunqi* (魂气, soul energy). So do [humans], so do birds, foxes and other animals, so do stones, rivers, and mountains, so do the stars and the moon! *Hun-qi* is everywhere. It can go up or down, flow or wander, enter or leave, hide or manifest itself! At the same time, it can be touched; and it exists forever and never dies. Divinity is not mysterious! One who has *hun-qi* has it. Possessed by *hun-qi*, one is *shushen* (属神, part and parcel with spirit, possessed by a spirit and controlling the spirit); one is *lingshen* (领神, spokesperson for god or spirit).

Finally, a shaman's inspired utterances of the Seven Hulun Clans from the sixteenth year of Qing Emperor Guangxu's reign[7] says, "Shen is the home of energy. A shaman who uses energy has spirit, or more clearly, spiritual powers."

The aforementioned ways of understanding divinity or spirit are not just those of the Manchu and their Jurchen ancestors; they are representative of the ideologies of all northern shamanic ethnic peoples. From these excerpts, we can sum up several points. First of all, shamanism considers that the notion of deity or spirit stems from human thinking. Godly beings exist in all things around us. Different from the beliefs of some other religions, *shen* did not spring from nothing or attain divinity by ecstatic practices. Divinity is what human beings sense, perceive, and hope for in the objective world. To put it another way, spirit is the reflection of people's ideas. This understanding has a tendency towards simple materialism. Second, though shamans get in contact with the spirit world, their spiritual acts of magic, power, and divination are all attained through their own repeated practice. They become superhuman by gathering the energy and power of all in this way and are the wise and powerful people of the clan. Third, according to shamanism, each shaman has magical power, but it admits that there are spiritual beings in the universe that can live in eternal separation from earthly living things and that bind together to exert their power on human beings to influence them to produce spiritual ideas or have spiritual experiences.

According to northern shamanism, too, the universe is filled with *qizhi* (气质, energy nature) or *qisu* (气素, energy essence). This mystic form of energy acts on humankind and all objective phenomena as a concrete form of spirit. All omens and manifestations of power are the result of its movement. The incarnation or communication of this energy, or *qi*, is prominent in shamanic thought and constitutes the heart of the operational laws of primordial shamanic spirits. The idea of divinity is actually this *qi*; it is a supernatural force that exists beyond the world of this earth. Shamans imitate, absorb, deploy and control it to cure disease, protect offspring, and predict the future. In a sense, to believe in this energy is thus to believe in spirit; it belongs to spirit. Vice versa, spirit is this energy. Spirit and energy produce and complement each other. They constitute the core power of all shamanic activities and the kernel dogma of shamanism. For this reason, my father and village elders emphasized the concept of *qiyun* (气运, energy motion) that they received from their elders. They would conduct augury sessions according to *qi-yun* to predict the harvest or the clan's fate and when an elder shaman passed away or when a *jiao'uyun* session was held to teach new clan shamans. So it is not an exaggeration to say that concepts concerning manifestations of *qi* are the oldest of all shamanic concepts handed down from generation to generation.

Qi is also embodied in the soul, as we shall see shortly. Ling Chunshen pointed out many years ago in *The Goldi Tribe on the Lower Sungari River (Songhuajiang xiayou de hezhezu)* that the primitive beliefs of the Hezhe (Goldi) include the belief

> in the basic idea that *qi* energy produces everything. They worship their ancestors because both humans and animals have souls; they worship spirits and ghosts because disasters are caused by them; and they worship nature because all natural things are governed by spirits.
>
> (Ling Chunshen 1934:102)

This view is accurate. It points to the fact that underlying shamanic worship is *shengqi* (生气, vitality), *qihua* (气化, energy incarnation), and *qixian* (气显, energy manifestation). The basic idea is that energy is the mother of all things.

Since ancient times, there have been philosophical discussions on the notion of *qihua*. Back in the time of the Eastern Han dynasty (206 BCE–220 CE), the Taoist Wang Chong (王充, 27–c. 97 CE) taught that "Imbibing this fluid or energy, [humans] are born; and they live as long as they keep it. By the fusion of the *qi* of heaven and earth, all things of the world are spontaneously produced" (Wang Chong 1974). Centuries later, in the Northern Song dynasty (960–1127), the Confucian moral philosopher and cosmologist Zhang Zai (张载, 1020–1077) stated in *Changes and Correcting Ignorance* (*Zhengmeng*: *Taihe*) that "In the great void, there needs must be *qi*, or energy, which comes together to produce all things." Still later in Southern Song times (1127–1279), Cheng Yi (程颐, 1033–1107) writes,

> All things were born from *qi*, or energy. They then gathered together and took shape and came to be mutually affected and transformed under certain circumstances. As the shape of *qi* became more and more extended, it gradually dispersed and finally vanished from sight.

On the whole, in ancient China, *qi* means destiny, and "What humans can feel but not see is *qi*." Energy motion (*qiyun*) or energy manifestation (*qixian*) is the *qi*-transformed state of a human body or the cosmos. In the context of divination, it is fate or destiny. The Song dynasty work *History of Song* (*Songshi*) states that "Since heaven and earth became separated, all *qi* has been destined." Accordingly, divination aims to determine the destined state of things.

In original shamanist thought, it is believed that all things in the universe have their origin in an extremely subtle substance which appears and disappears, increases or decreases, not unlike these philosophical notions of *qi* and the ideas in the *Book of Changes*. In my opinion, these ancient concepts of *qi* originally had a certain materialist bent. They are the fruit of a naïve understanding of the world held by people in primordial tribal society. Later, that view of the world evolved into a kind of philosophical theory as it came to be accepted and improved on by the different levels of literati. The primeval ideology of shamanism, however, has remained almost unchanged throughout the ages, with no literary emendations. Its theological notions are thus not as profound or rigorous as the theories of Taoism, Confucianism, or Buddhism, but its religious understanding of energy incarnation (*qihua*) has greater value as a primal ideological system of unique cultural significance. Although Manchu, Oroqen, Hezhe, Daur, Eastern Mongol, Xibe, Ewenki and other northern shamans differ in their supernatural experiences when possessed by the spirits, all of them have claimed to the me that the speaking of a spirit to them in a possessed state is a matter of "receiving spirit energy" and that a shaman embodies "energy motion."

Whom the spirit chooses depends first and foremost on one's personal *qi* or energy. Shamans say that anyone may be chosen by the spirit if they "love contemplation," "have a tranquil mind," and "keep their energy alive." Many who have such qualities are young married women. Manchus chosen by the spirit have to undergo shaman training called *jao'uyun*. To invoke the spirits, tribespeople cleanse themselves and burn incense and spirit papers around the would-be shaman until they feel dizzy. In such a trance, they see phantom spirits and hear strange sounds or whisperings from nowhere. As the initiation process progresses, the person understands what the whisperings mean. If the process is successful, the person gains *qi*, hears a god's orders and instructions, and becomes a shaman. The more a shaman prays, the greater power they will get, sometimes eventually becoming a megashaman, with their own characteristic features and receiving much veneration. Such a great shaman lays much stress on practices focused on the energies of parts of the body to master the skill of *qi* motion and *qi* manifestation. In a sacrificial rite, they will feel at ease in spite of carrying objects up to several hundred kilograms for days and nights. Without eating or drinking, the shaman still has abundant energy, keen eyesight, and a sober mind, all of which keep tribespeople in awe. In shamans' terms, they are the marks of *qi*, energy motion (*qiyun*), or energy essence (*qisu*) that are attained through long-time practice. When praying to a deity, shamans may demonstrate supernatural abilities as evidence of their unique energy – walking on fire coals or a bed of nails, diving deep down into a stream, lifting a great weight, uprooting a tree, flying away, springing up high, descending into a gorge, putting on red-hot foot gear, rolling about on needles, or handling razor-sharp blades. They say that the supernatural energy does not come from within themselves but rather is awakened by the external force of *shenqi* (神气, spirit energy) and can be summoned to help with a particular task. It may give one either godly or demonic power, but if the spirit energy weakens or decays, the shaman will come to naught and can never serve as a medium again.

Also according to shamanism, if the external spirit energy disappears, it does not really die; it plants itself in another possessed person, who in turn becomes the tribe's shaman as external and internal energies blend together to serve the people. This is the cycle of shamanic incarnation. Many veteran shamans can thus invoke the spirits of earlier shamans. People call this possession by a past shaman. This inheritance continues age after age as the *qi* of shamanhood is passed down. Shamans bodily pass away, but the *qi* gets passed down to the next generation.

In the past, many scholars took all this as sheer superstition and looked down on it. However, Chinese research in recent years has found that *qi*-like energy indeed circulates in the human body (Sun and Li 2004:11–12). I believe that *qi* energy and supernatural power not only exist now but were present in old times as well. However, there is need for further study. The existence of a soul is another key aspect of ancient shamanist ideas about spirits. The shamanist religion claims that all things have their souls and that humans have three souls. First, there is the life soul (*minghun*, 命魂). Any living thing possesses this soul. When a creature is alive, this soul exists; when the creature dies, it ceases to exist. In this world, human beings depend mainly on this soul. The second is the floating soul (*fuhun*, 浮魂). It manifests itself as the dream soul (*menghun*, 梦魂) or the will soul (*yinianhun*, 意念魂) and is limited only to humans and high-level beasts, birds, and insects. It may exist independently or wander out of the body to contact other living beings. The activity of this soul governs a human being's thirst for knowledge and is the source of willpower and the supernatural power of augury, mystic intuition, and wise foretelling, but it can also be affected by the external world and be a hidden source of temptation. In some rituals, the shaman draws the light of the heavens or the sun onto a sacred object, and if they fix seven-coloured sunbeams onto a person, they will make a fool wise or a coward brave. The third is the spiritual soul (*shenhun*, 神魂) or the true soul (*zhenhun*,真魂). This soul may lie hidden in the teeth, bones, or hair. It is eternal, the base of all the three souls, and in its incarnated state, it vitalizes humans and other animals. Shamans argue that though the body decays soon after a person dies, they can still invoke this true soul and talk with it.

The three-soul theory (*sanhun lun*, 三魂说) is found in all branches of northern shamanism – essentially the same ideology but with different names. Some Altaic and Yakut terms for soul are "*teng*" and "*kute*," and terms for life are "*sunei*" and "*suer*." Deep down, each living creature has a *teng* soul, and once it leaves, the person dies. There is also *kute* in every living creature, and where there is *kute*, its host is rich and their livestock thriving. Once it occupies the herder's whip, no disease or wolf dare attack the herd. *Sunei*, however, is unique to humankind. Like the floating soul above, *sunei* makes humans think, feel, and desire, and when one falls asleep, it leaves the body to wander around. Here the human soul, in particular that of a dead person, knows how to communicate with all other souls and minor spirits and can transmigrate into another soul, and souls of the dead desire to possess a living person's body. Shamans are commonly asked to seek out the soul of a dead person or animal in the other world. Through long-learned efforts, they can then return to the human world when summoned and possess a spirit idol. Such idols thus give comfort to the Manchu and other northern peoples; they are believed to be alive and watch over the clan or tribe day and night.

Shamanism believes that the soul, also called soul energy (*hunqi*, 魂气), is a *qi*-like substance. Folk legends imagine it as a kind of yellowish brown or murky black mist that has ever-changing forms. At one time, it may look like an oval bubble that rolls along a leaf or blade of grass like a bead of water. At another time, it may float in the air like a black bird or gallop like a horse. It is thus often referred to as a child soul (*tongzihun*,童子魂). In any case, it is visible only to shamans or people with special sight, who can often see the floating souls, in particular those of the newly deceased. However, soul energy is often mistaken for its materialized form. In general, according to shamanism, various spirit energies move about in the cosmos, including those of humans and animals. This is the basis for spirit worship, belief in ghosts, and belief that shamans can act as spirit mediums.

One may ask what the differences between soul energy and the energy incarnation (*qihua*) mentioned earlier are. Energy incarnation refers to the energy motion (*qiyun*) of *qi*-energized forces within all natural beings, mostly within living animals and plants. On the other hand, soul energy refers to the energized form of dead humans or animals in the form of the floating souls (*fuhun*) or true souls (*zhenhun*) spoken of earlier. In fact, soul energy is the *qi* of ghosts. Energy incarnation and soul energy are thus two aspects of the spirit force of beings of nature – the one of the living, the other of the dead. In early shamanism, ghosts were regarded as a kind of spirit, with no distinction between ghosts and spirits. Ghosts were one kind of spirit, and demonic ghosts were spirits that brought about harm and are thus referred to as evil spirits in some oracles. In any case, depending on whether they are spirits of the dead or those of the living, souls manifest themselves through energy incarnation or soul energy, and shamans offer sacrifice to the spirits in terms of how much *qi* they manifest.

Different spirits fall into different cultic groupings according to a particular shaman's command over of energized spirits, soul energies, and ghosts. Although the ethnic peoples of northern China have some common deities, each has its own pantheon of gods and guardian spirits in accordance with its particular living conditions and customs, and objects of worship vary widely. Worship centres mainly on bird, wolf, deer, and fish deities or on a plait of shaggy hair.

Bird cult shamans usually decorate their ritual headdress with carved eagles, with the number of eagles representing the rank of divinity. The Manchu, their Jurchen ancestors, and the linguistically related Xibe have traditionally decorated their headdresses with bird-shaped ornaments. As many as twenty-seven such ornaments may adorn the headdress of the highest ranked shaman, and falcons or condors embossed on its edges make it mighty and awe-inspiring.

The cult of the wolf is the posterity of Turkic and Mongol peoples, with most of the ethnic groups that worship the wolf doing so because it is the god of the prairie (*Caoyuan zhi shen*). Their shamans commonly wear a headdress ornamented with a wolf paw, tail, and skull. They say that wolf bone and fur produce a hallucinogenic scent and that taking whiffs of it draws one into a ritual trance, under the influence of which they may do what no one has ever done before.

In tribes of the deer cult, deer antlers represent the chief shaman, with the number of tines on the headdress indicating the rank of shamanic divinity and cultic group. Such tribes are often primordial tribes of North and Northeast Asia, especially forest peoples. As can be known from artefacts and conversations with veteran shamans, this is a long tradition. It is said that the earliest headdress insignia were wild beast bones or horns but that later they came from various local animals, including, according to recent excavations, broken mammoth teeth. As later ethnic groups evolved, wild beasts were driven away to distant mountains, and deer antlers began to be used – delicate, light, and handsome. As time went by, this became the common folk custom. Some Manchu clans have used them, whereas others have preferred bird ornaments.

Fish cults were often seen among Indigenous people on Sakhalin Island and the Amur Estuary. Ornaments for their shamanic headdresses are fish bones and skins and fish-skin beads. Their shamans often worship sea and river deities, especially the East Sea goddess, who has a fish head and woman's body. She is thought to govern light, warmth and water and has the duty of sending these precious gifts to the human world, along with the seven-coloured rays of the sun and fresh dew. As is typical of shamanic water spirits, only a few can fly.

As I have said, one cult centres on a plait of shaggy hair in the shaman's headdress. The brim of the headdress is trimmed with cloths of seven colours or leather or iron. The plait is made by intertwining a woman's hair with caudal bristles and the beard of a seal or sealion. The shaman wears long hair drooping over their shoulders and decorates their forehead with bone or stone beads and the like. Sometimes a string of bones from a bird's neck or around the eyes of a fish is also used. Shamans of several northern peoples have used such a headdress. Buryat shamans often dress themselves like a beggar seeking blessings from the gods. They are called *qiuqi* shaman and are thought to have divine status far beyond others.

Finally, there is also the worship of the demonic ghosts mentioned earlier. This is a rather recent phenomenon; it was not part of the original worldview of northern shamanic cultures but rather a product of Han culture, with its witches and Taoist ideology. Under Han influence, lords of the underworld and ghosts came to be absorbed into the shaman pantheon. Nevertheless, this cannot be ignored.

1.4 The multilayered shamanic world

The ancient idea of multiple heavens was the cornerstone of fledging shamanism in the north, and in the pantheon of northern shamanism, the gods of heaven have always held an eminent place. The global academic community has put great efforts into studying the ancient multiple heavens concepts and notions of heavenly deities. Some Chinese scholars have argued that "the god of heaven as a comprehensive concept appeared very late" (Qiu Pu 1985:19), but this does not agree with the worship of heaven found in the rites of northern ethnic peoples. In accordance with first-hand investigations of the shamanic heritage of the region and Manchu shaman's inspired utterances, I think that shamanic worship of the celestial being is a time-honoured tradition and that it is essentially different from the worship of deified emperors that arouse after the emergence of class society. The worship of heavenly forces of nature is based on the concept held by primordial human beings that natural phenomena and forces are strong-willed, living beings. The most prominent heavenly objects worshipped in northern shamanism are those that have close ties with humans – the sun, the moon, wind, snow, thunder, lightning, hail, and so on and influence peoples' daily lives. In the minds of early human beings, the divine world has a profound influence on the human world, and divine beings may come into this world, dwell in anything, and play dominant roles. Any social change or natural phenomenon beyond human control was thus considered the work of divine forces. In Chinese, the generic name for these forces is expressed in the ideographic character *tian* (天, heaven), which the 121 CE Han dynasty dictionary *Interpretation of Characters* (*Shuowen jiezi*) translates as "the great supreme being." The most eminent shamanist deities are the unfathomable, unbounded heaven and the fleeting heavenly forces of wind, thunder, and lightning: those that kept primordial human beings in awe. The worship of heavenly deities was surely an initial notion of shamanic belief.

Early myths speak of the chaos of the primordial cosmos. Among the Savage Jurchen of the far north lower-middle reaches of the Amur, one of three Jurchen groups noted in the Ming dynasty (1368–1644), the widespread Manchu shamanic myth "War in Heaven" (*Tiangong dazhan*) says of the primordial chaotic world that "A long, long time ago, there was no materialized heaven. It flowed like flood waters and floated like clouds." The heaven and earth were too dense to be separated, and heaven had not yet taken supremacy over the earth. As with other ancient notions of the primordial universe, in this myth heaven had no fixed form, let alone divinity. Norse myths express a similar belief that the universe was originally in sheer chaos – no heaven, no earth, no sea (Mao Dun 1929:17). Similarly, an ancient Chinese text states that "The world in chaos was thick like an egg" – a simple shamanic metaphor of the primordial heaven as an embryo, with flowing water and clouds symbolizing heaven's movements. Some Manchu inspired shamanic utterances express ancient peoples' sense of the vastness of heaven with the poetic expression, "The blue sky is lofty and unbounded," and the oracles of some tribes speak of heaven as the dwelling of Sūn Morin, the sun horse. With a feeling of the awe that surrounds ancients' worship of celestial beings, still other oracles celebrate the multicoloured clouds in the sky as "acts of gods or spirits," "things transformed by spirits," and "the movement of the spirits."

Ancient mythic interpretations of the structure of the world of heaven vary in line with the observations of different northern peoples, and this gave rise to a multitude of oracles. One Manchu oracle says, "Rising up in the clouds, one finds that the heaven has ninety-nine levels, each inhabited by different spirits." The Japanese researcher Akamatsu Chijyo discovered an inspired shamanic utterance in North Korea who claims that the universe "has thirty-nine divine worlds" (Akamatsu Chijyo 1938). Some Turkic shamans have thought that "there are thirty-three heavenly worlds. Tuvans of southern Siberia also have a belief in thirty-three heavens. Manchu shamans commonly think of heaven as divided into nine levels, the nine realms of the divine cosmos, with "nine" meaning simply "very many" or "infinite." Other northern ethnic groups have had similar notions.

In general, the cosmos is thought to have multiple, even countless, heavens. Russian scholar N.A. Aleksyev speaks of a Yakut shaman who had to stop to take many breaks – to be accurate, thirty-nine – before visiting the great spirit of the cosmos Urutoiweng. In line with the Yakut tradition of the worship of heaven, many veteran shamans have taught the art of *oyon*, a shamanic term that means "spinning the soul thrice to ascend to heaven." A shaman makes turns, commonly three, to leave their body and go up to the heaven in trance. In the past, a shaman had to work hard to pass this tribal test. If one does not pass, one could not be a true shaman and deserve the divine title, but if one passes, one can act as spirit medium who serves the tribe by knowing oracles and conveying prayers to the gods.

In the minds of Manchu and other northern peoples, the cosmos is imagined as a cosmic tree. Legend has it that this tree is at the centre of the cosmos and connects all sub-universes. Its roots are the underworld, the trunk the intermediate world, and its seven or nine branches the worlds of divinities. This metaphor reflects an early view of the cosmos when human thinking was only budding. It dates back far earlier than the number-based expression of the various levels of the cosmos, and it has influenced the thought of all the shamanic peoples of China, Siberia, and Northeast Asia. In accordance with this concept, the Manchu erect their sacred pole and the Mongols set up the *oboo*, a ritual heap of stones or wood piled up at a mountain pass or highland, with willow branches stuck in it.

The shamanic multiple heaven view of ancient slave and feudal societies and the so-called feudal society of late Qing dynasty was at various times influenced and infiltrated by Buddhism, Tibetan Lamaism, and Christianity. In particular, when the ruling class of the early Qing dynasty sought to promote the standardization of sacrificial rites, they introduced into shamanic rituals nonshamanic deities such as Avalokiteśvara and sagacious lord Guan Yu, the great general of the late Eastern Han dynasty who died in 220 EC and has been popularly revered for his loyalty and bravery. The multiple heaven view has continued in northeastern shamanism, but the primitive concepts of heaven have faded out, and the theory of three realms (*Sanjie Shuo*, 三界说) has widely spread. As stated in the encyclopaedic opus *Classified Qing Anecdotes* (*Qingbai leichao*) compiled by Qing scholar Xu Ke (徐珂) and published in 1917, "Shamanism established the concept of three realms: the first, Upper Realm, is paradise; the second, Middle Realm, is earth; the third, Lower Realm, points to Hell or the Underworld" (Xu Ke 1984:63–64). The Upper Realm is the abode of the deities, the Lower Realm is dominated by the devil, and the Middle Realm is inhabited by human beings. Xu Ke's account is based on North Asian and Nordic shamanic ideas. Of the Ewenki in Siberia, it is said that

> In light of the shamanic symbolic cosmos of the Ewenks, there are three realms of the universe: the Upper World in the east, from which the shamanic Endekit River rises; the Middle World, namely the river itself; and the Lower World in the north. The mighty cosmic river has many branches, and each branch also has sub-branches, each the domain of a particular shaman. Later the Upper World was believed to be a realm of a deity called Xeweji, Aike-saili, or Mayin, along with unborn souls, or *aomidai*. The lower reaches of the river world is that of dead souls.
>
> (Guo Yanshun and Sun Yunlai 1983:92–93)

Buddhism also has the concept of three cosmic realms, but they are understood differently: the Realm of Sensuous Desire for humans, the Realm of Form for semi-gods, and the Realm of Formlessness for pure spirits. The second realm has many heavens. Unlike shamanism, Buddhism preaches ideas of emptiness such as *karma* and meditative concentration. Xu Ke's account is widely divergent from this Buddhist concept.

Comparing the three realms view with the more original multiple heaven view helps us recognize how human thinking in the area has evolved. As the numeric abstraction of the universe evolved from multiple heavens to three realms with the development of society, northern shamanism became more hybrid, and its cosmos became richer and more vivid. It incorporated ideas of diverse nature such as the supreme being of Christianity and the Orthodox Church, Buddhist *karma* and Lord Yama, and the five emperors of the Taoist netherworld. The Yakut notion of three realms, for example, was possibly influenced by Protestantism or Eastern Orthodox ideas. Quite a few ethnic groups came to believe in the existence of hell. The Hezhe have thought that the Upper World is heaven, the Middle World is this mortal world, and the Lower World is the abode of monsters and demons, whose duty is to punish sinners. According to Mongol shamanism, the Upper World is inhabited by divine beings who often fight to protect mortals from the forces of hell that spread plagues and disasters throughout the human world (Lin Chunsheng 1934:103). There is also an unknown realm between the Middle World and the

Lower World which the dead inhabit. For their part, Turkic peoples, as reported by Japanese scholar Shibata Kenzo in *A Record of Manchu Religions* (*Manzhou zongjiao zhi*), have believed in Dange Karahan, the good heavenly spirit, who is like Jesus Christ in Christianity. This deity partitioned the cosmos into the world of light and the world of darkness of human beings. Heaven is the world of gods and spirits, while hell abounds with demons and ghosts (Liu Jianguo 1981:120).

Handwritten shaman's inspired utterances that I collected suggest that the three-realm view has prevailed in the shamanist cultures of the Nordic peoples and the peoples of North and Northeast Asia and that the more traditional nine-heaven view has dominated the northeast of China, but with influences of the three-realm concept. The Manchu concept is the richest and most mythological of all, embellished with tales of subduing demons and monsters. In the mythic tale Nishan Shaman, a shamaness descends to the Lower World at the request of an elderly couple to meet the lord of the underworld Erleg Khan and bring back the soul of their young son. In the myth "Nine Heavens in the Three Realms" ("Jiutian sanjie"), the Manchu cosmos has the traditional nine levels, but they are separated into three realms. The highest three levels comprise the realm of heaven: the heavenly realm, the realm of fire, and the realm of light. There dwell the supreme god of heaven, Abka Enduri, and other deities, along with many animal and plant spirits and deceased heroes. In portrayals collected from many clans, there are two divine birds that govern the sun at the left and the moon at the right and that glow with dazzling light throughout heaven. The realm of the middle three levels is for humans, birds, animals, and lesser sprites. The realm of the lowest levels is that of the netherworld. It is the home of the earth mother Banaji Emu, night-watching female spirits, and the devil Yeluli. As messengers of the nine heavens, shamans can fly up to the skies to converse with deities in the realm of heaven, subdue unwholesome spirits in the human realm, and descend to the dark place, where they sweep away all the demons but also invoke Banaji Emu for a good harvest and abundance across the land.

The complex cosmic concept of the Manchus and their Jurchen ancestors maintains the original idea that heaven and earth are in somewhat chaotic communion. Their earthly realm is not Buddhist hell, but it includes demons and troublesome sprites, and as we know from the Manchu creation myth "War in Heaven," the demon Yeluli can rush up to the heaven and make havoc there. That is quite a dialectical idea, and no divisions are absolute. Everything complements everything else. Plagues, disasters, and misfortunes frequently befall the human world, and the underworld is the home not only of evil spirits but also of divine beings like Banaji Emu. The birth of these ideas is bound up with ancient peoples' custom of dwelling in caves. As is said in the 445 CE *Book of Later Han* (*Houhan shu*) by Fan Ye (范晔), "cave dwellers may climb down nine ladders to descend below." This living pattern led them to worship earthly spirits and spirits of the underground. This idea is not limited to the Manchu. Indigenous people in the Arctic have also believed that there is world deep in the underground that is not the exclusive domain of darkness and evil: "It enjoys more beautiful sunshine than above ground, and it feels like summer all the year round" (Jin Qicong 1986). All this forms the totality of the multidimensional framework of the multiple heaven shamanist world of northern China.

Notes

1 Qianlong 乾隆 (1711–1799). His sixty-year reign was marked by cultural and economic prosperity, during which Manchu language genealogies, histories, ritual handbooks, the *Shamanic Code*, and the *Complete Books of the Four Imperial Libraries* 《四库全书》 were compiled.
2 The Oroqen 鄂伦春 are ethnic people in northern China who live mainly in the Inner Mongolia autonomous region and Heilongjiang. They are traditionally mainly hunters and customarily use animal fur and skins for clothing. They believe in shamanism.
3 The Daur 达斡尔 are ethnic people of northern China who live mainly in the Morin Dawa Daur autonomous banner, Hulun Buir, and the Inner Mongolia autonomous region, but some live near Tacheng in the Xinjiang Uygur autonomous region. They belong to the Mongol branch of the Altaic linguistic family and believe in shamanism.
4 The Ewenki 鄂温克 are ethnic people of northern China who live mainly in Heilongjiang and the Inner Mongolia autonomous region. They belong to the Manchu-Tungus branch of the Altaic linguistic family and believe shamanism.
5 The Hezhe 赫哲族 are ethnic people in China and are known as Nanai in Russia and formerly as Golds, Goldes, Goldi, or Samagir. Traditionally living by fishing and hunting along the Amur, Sunggari, and Ussuri rivers, they believe in shamanism and have a rich oral literature known as *yimakan*.
6 In Chinese philosophy, *yin-yang* refers to how opposite or contrary forces are actually complementary, interconnected, and interdependent in the natural world and how they give rise to each other as they interrelate.
7 Guangxu 光绪(1871–1908) is the eleventh Qing emperor, who reigned from 1875 to 1908, but in actual reality from 1889 to 1898 and under Dowager Empress Cixi's 慈禧 influence. He initiated the Hundred Day's Reform but was abruptly stopped when she launched a coup in 1898 and put him under house arrest until his death.

2 Nature worship

According to the world view of the Udege people, "There is nothing without life in nature or the cosmos. Everything is a living being, alive like humans. Even the earth itself is a gigantic living creature" (Arsenyev 1983:305). This is in line with the idea of the polytheistic shamanism of the peoples in northern China. In the eyes of primordial tribal groups, their celestial and secular worlds were inhabited by a variety of deities and spirits who were of different functions and statuses, good or evil. As a German poet said centuries later, "In every tree, there is a spirit breathing now. The world seen by our eyes is full of holy spirits" (Heine 1974:21). In the traditional shamanic view, the entire cosmos, is a paradise of countless spirits (*shen*) to whom shamans address their prayers. The roots of religious belief sprung from the weakness we experienced in the times when nature did not support our life needs. In any case, striving to survive and have a peaceful life, primeval human beings spontaneously worshipped nature. In northern shamanism in China, each clan commonly had its own spirit deities who lived in harmony with one another, not encroaching on one other's authority. Some personified natural forces, though humanlike, and were actually animals and plants. Still others were idols or figurines that symbolized forces of life, and some were great clan ancestors who contributed much to the clan, of which clan protective deities were most prominent.

2.1 Nature deities

In the early shamanism of northern China, multiple materialized forms were piously believed to be spirits. At the earliest stage of shamanism, people thought that everything had a soul. Their worship of nature began with natural phenomena and later came to involve human and half-human spirits. Nature worship focused on figures that may seem rather strange but that are strongly symbolic. A rock or cliff is drawn simply in miniature, for example, to represent a mountain: , as often be found on shamanic costumes, headdress, and ritual vessels. Water lines are also commonly seen on shamanic costumes at the bottom of a shaman's ritual skirts . For their part, straw, fur, or cloth strips symbolizing wind are woven into shamanic costumes as , some sewn together with hundreds or even thousands of colourful ornaments.

In the shamanic world, all things have souls, and as long as wandering souls are represented on ritual garments or objects, a shaman can offer prayers to an object of nature anywhere and anytime.

The sun, moon, and stars enjoy the highest reverence in nature worship. Adoration of the sun dates back early in the history of northern shamanism. This is because ancient tribes in the cold north had a dread of natural forces like frost, ice, and snow, which they regarded as threats to humans and other creatures. A snowstorm can destroy all mountain life overnight. Northern shamanism thus attaches great importance to the sun god. When the first day of the first lunar month comes, northern peoples have a long-standing custom of venerating the east, where the sun rises. The Oroqen have called the sun Derecin, a supreme being. A story narrated in 13th-century *The Secret History of the Mongols* (*Menggu mishi*) says, "I dreamed of a great white falcon bearing the sun and the moon with its claws into my hands" (Tsendin Damdinsüren 1956:41).[1] On the basis of oracle tales of the Manchu Fuca Hala (clan), the first shaman was brought from the east by a white falcon whose paws held a dazzling stone called *dunen* (brilliant sun), which was actually the soul of the sun. Later, the *dunen* evolved into a plurality, *dunensi* (myriad brilliant suns).[2] For this reason, a shaman always wears many glistening crystals and small bronze mirrors (*tori* in Manchu). According to veteran shamans' ancestral records, the mirrors symbolize the bright sun and are rare treasures that can dispel all evils, show demons' true colours, and point the path to divinity.

Among emblems of the sun, moon, and stars, the sun mirror is the largest. A shaman commonly wears two mirrors during a ritual performance, the larger on the chest and the other on the back, which signifies bearing the sun and the moon respectively. Another two mirrors are placed at both shoulders – the sun to the left and the moon to the right – and still another two are hung on the front and back of the waist to indicate mutual, eternal shining. In addition, every part of the shaman's costume is inlaid with small mirrors, stringed clam shells, stones, bones, horns, and fish gills. Shamanic tales say that celestial bodies were transformed from polished mirrors scattered about by the spirits, so such bodily ornaments are naturally associated with the stars of the cosmos. Most of the personified deities of northern shamanic natural worship are female, and shamanic myth says that the celestial stars are all female. The sun, in Manchu language *sūn*, is the eldest sister; Biya (moon) is the second sister; white clouds are next, and stars are other younger sisters. Together they constitute a huge female celestial family. Even a male shaman has to dress like a shamaness; otherwise, he cannot be in trance. The female celestial concept manifests the ancient shamanic lineage of female supremacy that goes back to the matriarchal age. The mirrors on the shaman's costume reflect the fact that in old times men often covered only their privates and buttocks, and the mirror covering the crotch refers figuratively to female fertility and fertility worship, as will be discussed later.

As society marched forth, fishing and hunting peoples formed the idea that a divine animal governs the sun. In the Manchu heroic epic *Umesiben Mama*, the story of the shamaness chieftain Umesiben, who unified the Donghai Jurchen ancestors of the Manchus, the sun is *sūn morin*, a horse running the course of the day, and Manchu myth regards it as a white horse with radiant flames that runs so fast that no one dare see its light. Another ethnic group represents it as a running deer, and Han people believe it is a divine bird that flies time and time again. According to an early Manchu shamanic myth, the venerable mother sun, called Sūn Anbo Mama, has fiery hair as long as the nine (myriad) heavens. It flows down to earth and illuminates it with vibrant light. The mother sun lives in the nine heavens, busily dispatching minor spirits to the earth, in particular as the spirit who became the first shaman. The story says that long, long ago, she ordered the eagle deity to nurse a baby girl and bring her up to be a powerful shaman. So a shaman is the sun's daughter, and as we have said, the mirrors on shaman garments are metamorphosed as the light from the sun. The story continues as follows:

> The wind deity Sisilin is a powerful deity who can devour everything with his broad mouth. He is a womanizer as well, and many females wanted to be his wife. The sun, however, flatly denied his approaches, so he always chased after her. Running all the time, she left him far behind. Sisilin got furious and blew away the sun from her sister the moon, so that the two sisters could never meet each other again. When the sun came out, everything bloomed, but when it hid from the wind, the icy earth became lifeless.

Shamanist believers have commonly offered blood sacrifice to the wind deity, who would devour the blood, mistake it for the sun, and stop chasing the sun. The sun could thus come out again.

Sun worship has first place in shamanism because its light and heat were indispensable. Moon worship comes second. The moon was considered a "very kind, tender sister," and tales about the moon deity flourished once the sense of the yearly seasons came to the fore with improved methods of agriculture. Northern myths see the moon as the deity of the hunt, as a goddess patrolling the night, or as a huge lantern illuminating the night.

There is also the cloud deity Ili Gege of the Manchu and Ilan Tusu of other northern peoples, such as the Oroqen, Daur, Ewenki, Hezhe, and Xibe.[3] The cloud deity is a graceful, attractive goddess. Although fairly obstinate, as a sister of Sūn Anbo Mama, she protected the spirit princess Sūn Gege. The cloud goddess is clever at making bridges and tents out of clouds and using them to beautify the sky. She usually travels around the heavens quietly with many wandering fairies and elves clinging to her colourful attire. In the Manchu creation myth of the Heishui (Black River) Jurchen tribes, "War in Heaven," however, she blocked Sisilin in his chase after the sun. The sky became a maze that the sky goddess Abka Hehe created to entrap the demon Yeluli, and if a shaman wants to ascend to the sky, they need to use clouds as wings or a ladder of stars or bright sunbeams. Shaman garments must have cloud patterns, which are said to have been brought into use by the first shaman from heaven.

In "War in Heaven," the beautiful goddess Nimanggi Mama or Xangyan Mama helps Abka cover the earth with her white vapour to make the dark evil demon

Yeluli materialize. Sūn Gege directs strong beams of light at him, and Nimanggi's son Bonoku punches him. Yeluli has no choice but to run away into the depths of the earth and is finally defeated. Nimanggi Mama is the snow deity, and her son Bonoku the hail deity. For peoples in the North, snow was neither a threat nor a disaster but an intimate friend. Snow could bring them everything – a house, a tent, skis, and a cellar for storing food and sheltering themselves from wild beasts. So it is no small wonder that snow is personified as holy mother.

In northern shamanism, the worship of the sky or heaven (*tian*天) goes back to the matriarchal era when many deities were females. It embraces all of the natural phenomena associated with the sky: clouds, fog, dew, snow, rain, thunder, frost, hail, mist, rainbows, stars, and so on. In the traditions of northern peoples, it finds expression mainly in two systems, depending on the two main names of the sky god: Abka for the Manchu, Hezhe and Xibe peoples of the Manchu language family, and Tenggeri for the Mongol and Daur of the Turkic family. Other appellations are Buwasong in the Ewenki (Solon) language and Wujichu in Oroqen. Although the worship of heaven involves the worship of everything that appears in the sky, it cannot be compared with the divinity of later monotheistic religions. Moreover, heaven and the heavenly deities are quite different. Neither is subordinate to the other, and the heavenly deities are all sisters who have equal status. The shamanic concept of sky or heaven in the matriarchal period is analogous to relationships within matriarchal society, and it became imbedded in people's consciousness as it evolved into a mythology of goddesses in a female family of divinities. The heavenly kingdom was thus a mirror of matriarchal society. For his part, the supreme male heaven deity Abka Enduri came into existence as society evolved forwards later and became patriarchal.

As society evolved, later Indigenous peoples came to express their sacrificial worship of heaven in more-ceremonious forms, and as can be seen from ritual documents and official histories, a system of rites began taking shape. Ever since the Mongols' rise in the northern steppes, they have kept the rite of worshipping Tenggeri, using simple ritual garments and clean sacrificial utensils. According to the *History of Yuan* (*Yuan shi*),[4] the emperor and empress would always attend the rite, along with other royalty. On the eighth day of the eighth month of the second year of his reign (1252), Emperor Möngke Khan[5] worshipped heaven (Tenggeri) at Mount Riyue in sacrificial dress. On the twelfth day of the twelfth month, he decided to erect a sacrificial altar in the southeast, seven *li* (1 li = 0.5 km) from the Lizheng Gate (currently Qianmen) of the capital. Two tablets were set up for the supreme lord of heaven and imperial queen of earth, and the emperor would thereafter attend major rites there to offer sacrifice to heaven and earth (Song Lian 1975). The shamanic worship of nature and heaven highlighted the importance of mountain worship. According to the *History of Liao* (*Liao shi*),[6]

> For the Mountain Sacrifice, tablets are erected for the god of heaven and queen of earth toward the east at Muye Mountain. One tree is planted amid other trees to stand for the emperor surrounded by state ministers, and two other trees are planted to resemble a sacred gate. If a drought causes havoc,

> an auspicious day should be selected to hold a rite to ask for rain by shooting willow sprigs three times, twice by the emperor and once by each minister. For the rite to worship the sun, the emperor shall go up to the altar and kneel down twice on a cushion toward the Sun and then light incense sticks and insert them in the censer.
>
> (Toqto'a et al. 1975)

The *History of Jin* (*Jin shi*)[7] reads that "The Jin court followed the Liao rites for the worship of heaven on the Double Fifth Festival, the Hungry Ghost Festival, and the Double Ninth Festival" (Toqto'a et al. 1975).

The Qing dynasty (1644–1911) subsequently accepted all these past royal sacrificial rites, raising the rite to worship heaven to a new height. The records indicate that the worship of heaven was not merely a matter of worshipping nature; it included the concept of worshipping a supreme being. This points to shamanism's eventually becoming monotheistic, but that transition was still in its infancy, with many deities' still having equal status among them. The concept of a supreme being appeared much later.

Mountain worship emerged as clans developed from a fishing and hunting economy to a more complex system. To worship a mountain is, for any clan, to worship the place of their settlement. In the fledging fishing and hunting economy, people often moved from place to place, but with the advance of farming and hunting, they needed to attach themselves to mountains. Only then, when they settled down and lived by a mountain, could they think of worshipping it as a steep and lofty height which could inspire awe. Manchu clans believed that mountain deities were both male and female, and in the Qing dynasty, the mountain god was called Murin Murinhan and worshipped as the hunting god. Along with mountain worship, the nature worship of northern shamanism later led to the worship of animals and plants.

2.2 Totem deities

It has long been thought that there was no totem or fetish worship except from the Indigenous peoples in what is now called Australia, Mesopotamia, and what is now called North America. Instead, however, all primordial humans took to animals, plants, and phenomena of nature as totems in their worship of tribal ancestors, and even in modern times, the totem worship of natural forces can be found in Africa, Oceania, and Asia. It is also found among the northern peoples of China. Some scholars have denied this because no corresponding ancient symbolic figures have yet been discovered, but totem worship naturally sprang up in clan societies of people related by blood. Such peoples readily took animals, plants, or nonliving things as their logos or special protectors and thought of themselves as having special kinship with them. It can thus reasonably be argued that totemic figures existed in tribes and clans who believed in shamanism in northern China even though no artefacts have actually been discovered. An oracle of the Seven Hulun Clans[8] from the twenty-sixth year of the Qing dynasty Guangxu (光绪,

1875–1908) speaks of the existence of nine poles used in fire sacrifices with an antlered deer head, eagle head, bear head, and horned human face carved on them.

These odd-looking poles are not ordinary works of art; they are clan symbols with distinctive totemic implications. Sacred eagles, deer heads and antlers, leopard tails, and wolf tails are often found on clan shamans' headdresses. I argue that these animal ornaments are the equivalent of totemic logos and that they later became the group's mark of its deities. They were called *mafa* in the language of the Jurchen ancestors of the Manchu, meaning "ancestral god." Along with animals, plant totems have also been a vital force in Manchu shamanic culture. Willows, for example, have been an object of worship until present day. Perhaps as a reflection of the totemic awareness of an ancient stage of Manchu culture, they are associated with the female genitals as a fertility symbol, and they are the object of solemn lofty feelings of respect expressed by kneeling and peons of praise.

Scholars who doubt whether northern peoples have totem worship think that they could not have had so many totems or regarded plants and animals as totems. They overlook the hard fact, however, that tens of thousands of years have witnessed repeated separations, unifications, and interethnic fusions leading to the present mixed distribution of China's northern ethnic minority peoples. These peoples have become a mixture of ancient Turkic, Khitan, Mongol, and Jurchen tribes. Most Khitans interbred with Jurchens, and Jurchens are not pure bloodline descendants of their more ancient Sushen ancestors.[9] Before the formation of the Manchus, fusions had occurred among Jurchens, Hans, and Mongols, and in the late Ming (1368–1644) and early Qing dynasties, there were frequent fights, mergers, and divisions among interethnic groups, whose original beliefs ebbed and flowed with historical changes. It is hard to know what kinds of clan totems the ancient ancestors of present northern Chinese peoples had, but they surely varied greatly in style and functions that have been transmitted intact to this day as an indispensable aspect of their Indigenous shamanistic cultures.

One such totem is the bear, which is strongly enshrined among northern peoples. As Derevyanko has noted in *Tribes in the Amur River Basin*, "Some ancient tribes in the Far East often call the bear *amaha*, referring grandpa or dad, or in the forest *etihen, etihen*, meaning old man or uncle. Such names seem closely related with totemism" (Derevyanko 1987). The Ewenki traditionally call bears their grandpas and grandmas. The Oroqen's name for them is *nionioku*, but they never use that name directly; instead, they respectfully call the bear *amaha* (maternal uncle), *yaya* (grandfather), or *taitei* (grandmother). Traditionally, they paid tribute to the bear before it was butchered and pretended to cry after it was eaten. Some Manchu clans summoned the bear god in sacrificial rites, and some, such as the Seven Hulun Clans, painted it on their clan banners. Ancient tribes formed totemic groups that evolved into subtribes over the course of time. Their banner totems remained unchanged, which evokes a primordial feeling and adds to the complexity of shamanistic evolution. Bear worship has also enjoyed a long currency among Siberian peoples north of the Amur, such as the Buryat, Nivkh, Feiyaka, Ewenki (Nanai or Goldi), Hezhe, and Udege. Before killing a bear for meat, these ethnic groups celebrated a sacred bear rite, in which group members regaled themselves in joyous communion. They traditionally considered it their most grand festive rite, and those who got a share of the bear meat were believed to be protected and to remain invincible because the bear's invincible soul enters their body.

The northern peoples of Asia have had other totems as well, such as the wolf, leopard, birds, and fish. The Mongols, Oroqen, and others idolized the wolf with awe. The Oroqen named it *gusige* but venerated it as *weng*, an onomatopoeic term which sounds like a wolf's howling (Inner Mongolia Editorial Committee 1986c:52). The Manchu also offered sacrifices to the wolf god and painted it on their clan banner. The Ewenki traditionally worshipped a sort of grey heron (*galebule* in Tungus languages). They treasured it so much that neither shooting nor even scaring it away was allowed (Inner Mongolia Editorial Committee 1986b:341). Some Manchu clans paid special reverence to the eagle goddess, a mother deity with an eagle head and human body that has two huge breasts, a bulging belly, and a swollen vulva. Worshipped as the mother of the human race and the first shaman, she served as the protective deity of many Jurchen and later Manchu tribes, and I argue that she must have been their totem in the matriarchal age. Other ethnic groups, such as the Hezhe, have similar beliefs. Kori, the eagle deity in the Hezhe *yimakan*-style[10] creation epic evokes the invincibility of a shamaness. In that Hezhe story, the earliest human was *kade* or *huodai*; among the Oroqen, it was *huodou* or *hadou*, all transliterated in Chinese as *xuan niao* (玄鸟, bird of fantasy). *Kade* was male in Hezhe patriarchal society, but the deity retained vestiges of their original female forerunners.

Influenced by animism, northern fishing and hunting peoples have diversified rituals of shamanistic animal and plant worship. Manchu clans have beasts, birds of prey, or plants as deities, numbering up to seventy and ranging from land and marine mammals to small reptiles like frogs, lizards, and even snails. The various forms of worship passed down among them can never be thought to stem from totemism in a narrow sense; nor are they all derived simply from the prevalent matrilineal clan kinship of ancient times. Rather, their totemism appeared with the improvement and expansion of the livelihood methods of primordial people as they developed needs and fantasies for controlling and possessing the animals, waters, and grasslands of their areas. They thus came to enshrine pieces of the land with a sense of mystery. That is the origin of their nature worship. Fear, need, and desire can give rise to the worship of deities, and springing from such emotions, primordial shamanism came to include the worship of more and more deities, such that almost all living things were ultimately included. Of course, various tribes or clans have had different animal or plant deities in accord with their similar, but not identical, living conditions. Their worship of animals and plants is discussed throughout this book, but not independently in any particular chapter.

2.3 Fire worship

Fire is a great force of nature with a long history. It was cherished by human beings as soon as it was discovered and has played a huge role in human development. Fire worship was integral to northern shamanism, and fire sacrifices were offered to praise fire for its powerful service in dispelling cold, evil, and impurities and were offered as prayers for clan peace and prosperity. Fire worship originated from simple primordial nature rites of praying to heaven for warmth, light, and peace, and it has continued as an ancient custom among northern nationalities. As the famous Turkish scholar Abdülkadir Inan wrote in *Tarihte ve Bugün Şamanizm* (*Shamanism in History and Today*):

> Every shaman rite involves fire, and as a much-favored ritual, fire sacrifice has continued over a long period of time. Fire stunts were often performed when tribal-wide sacrifices were held. The scene was exciting and lively as tribesmen competed with one another in understanding, saving, setting and mastering fire. Elders would chant stories of the fire deity, and women exchanged their skills and taboos about using fire. All this reflects northern ancestors' heroic optimism.
>
> (Inan 1979)

According to records of the clan sacrifices of the Lang Hala in the Jin dynasty, the Jurchens used to sprinkle salt into the flames during a sacrifice, and if there was no salt, they used chips of wood. The sound of the crackling salt was taken as an auspicious omen. Moreover, a shaman would beat their drum, jangle their waist bells, and light a fire before a new house was built or the bride carried in. Fire was used, too, to burn out rats in the weeds in a custom known as chasing out ghosts (*qugui*,驱鬼). As the *History of Liao: Treatises of Rituals, Ritual on the Eve of the Spring Festival* (*Liaoshi lizhi suichuyi*) reads,

> In the early evening, ritual officiants along with court sacrificial attendants would come to the gate of the imperial palace. They put salt and mutton into a brazier fire, and shamans and mega shamans worshipped the fire deity in order. Lastly, ceremonial escorts would lead the emperor to worship the fire twice.
>
> (Toqto'a 1974)

The *History of Liao* also has a record of a ritual of "setting fire to sacrificial objects to offer worship to heaven" (Toqto'a 1974). Later, the Yuan dynasty held what was apparently the same ritual to worship heaven. A shaman would light a fire in a stone basin on the ground or in the courtyard. The ritual officiant would then butcher and flay a pig or sheep and scrape and wash the meat before roasting it as an offering to the deities.

Fire sacrifice was common among northern fishing and hunting tribes. *Legends of Nurhaci and Wanggao* (*Liangshi hanwang zhuan*) and *Records of the Grievances of the East Sea* give (*Donghai chenyuan lu*) offer a glimpse into the Jurchen hunting fire rite: the tribal chief would lead the tribespeople in deciding the location in the mountains for sprinkling wine and worshipping the god of the hunt. Then they would start shouting loudly and beating the rocks while setting fire all around. As the flames grew bigger, they all chased after wild beasts, and when the fire died out, they killed them and offered the nine largest ones to heaven. After scraping and washing the meat, they enjoyed eating the "heavenly fire meat." The Daur and Ewenki also had this custom. Sometimes called going fire hunting, it was actually a primitive mode of hunting.

According to traditional Manchu beliefs, to learn the past is to recall the past, and through play that imitates ancestral customs, people can learn and recall the past. In one ritual game, they light fires, and as the flames grow bigger, they play at chasing wild beasts. In another tradition, on the eve of the Spring Festival, they erect piles of firewood and foretell the peace of the coming year by huge bonfire. Manchu folklorist Zhao Wenjin (赵文金) recalled that the Manchu in former times had the custom of greeting the fire deity Tuwa Enduri to dispel evil. They kept an "eternal fire" alive and prohibited spitting into it, because for them it was holy, pure, and alive. In fact, they thought that something can be pure only after being torched or burnt.

Among the Mongols, the Zasag decree of Genghis Khan explicitly stipulates fire taboos. During the rite of alliance between the Jurchen King Wang Gao (王杲) and other chieftains, as well as between Wang Gao and the Gorlos Mongols, they sprinkled the blood of a black ox on a fire and then walked through the fire together. While being presented to Batu Khan, an envoy from Russia was ordered to walk through two fires to cleanse impurities. It was thought to be a great sin "to insert a knife in the fire, touch fire by any other means, pick a piece of meat from the pot or chop anything beside a fire" (Wu Yisang and Bagen 1987). For the Oroqen, the fire deity is called Tuowo Bukan. When having a meal, people would put some of the food into the fire as an offering. Splashing water on a fire and poking at a fire with a knife or fork were prohibited, so as not to infuriate the deity. A guest coming during the Spring Festival ought first to kneel to the fire deity and then wish the host a happy New Year. The Ewenki have traditionally venerated fire as a divine grannie, so women were prohibited from walking over fire, and when moving to a new dwelling, they dare not put out the hearth fire. They believed, moreover, that a wild fire breaks out by itself to dispel demons. The Daur thought that fire has a magical power to dispel evil or misfortune, so anyone returning from a funeral should walk over fire for good fortune and safety. The Hezhe call fire awe-inspiring Fojia Mama. There are similar customs and tales among the Ewenki (Nanai or Goldi), Hezhe, and Negidals of Russia and among the Indigenous people of what is now called Siberia. According to ancient Greek myths, moreover, Prometheus stole fire from heaven. Apollo, the god of fire and light and protector of hearth fires, was enshrined in a firepan. "He was the patron deity of families, cities and colonies as well as livestock" (Schmidt 1987:66). In ancient Greece, there was an eternal fire in the family home of each area chief or village head. It was a holy fire that maintained family and civic stability.

The worship of the hearth fire came into existence when humans began to settle down. So in general, fire deities emerged quite late, but not in northern China. For the northern peoples, age-old fire worship was integral to primordial shamanism. The fire deity was often female in the matriarchal society that flourished in northern China. As I have said, the Manchu fire deity is Tuwa Enduri (*eunduri* meaning "deity"), or fire mother goddess, *tuwa* and *emu* meaning respectively "fire" and "mother." She is called by that name in the Namdulu Hala and in other clans Tuwa Mama ("granny fire"). Manchu ancestors saw her as the mother for all living things, who rules over the light and heat of the cosmos and in some shamanic myths governs the rotation of seasons and the light and dark of the nine heavens. In sacrificial rituals, she traditionally has priority over the mountain, water, star, thunder, clouds, wind, and rain gods. Some Manchu oracles speak of her as a grannie in red whose garment was part of the sky. In ancient times, people believed that she lived in the highest realm of the sky vault and ran with the sun horse Sūn Morin day after day.

The various early shamanic fire deities reflect humankind's initial apprehension towards fire. To their way of thinking, it was utterly strange and inconceivable. It is not like natural food resources or water, which are visible in summer and winter. It is usually unseen. Oracles speak of fire as *edun angga* ("mouth of the wind" in Manchu). Keeping its mouth wide open, it can devour the forests and all living things. Verses from the Manchu shamanic epic *Umesiben Mama* read, "Fire comes smiling; fire comes jumping; fire comes from trees; fire comes from rain" (Fu Yuguang and Lu Liankun 2007). These verses indicate that the ancestors recognized that fire can crackle and torch things unexpectedly. Forests and rainstorms can easily break into fire.

The Mongol shamanic fire deity is also traditionally their Eji ("mother"); without her, a tribe can hardly live. They offered a yellow-headed white sheep to her with such words as "Khanum! Mother! My dear fire mother! Here we offer you butter, offer you a yellow-headed white sheep, offer you fat and oil, offer you *kefir* from mare's milk!" Peoples such as the Oroqen and Ewenki likewise took her as their Fojia Mama. All this gives evidence not only of reverence of fire but also of the high status that the female had in ancient matriarchal society. Fire worship was widespread in northern cultures because to fathom and master fire was for ancient human beings a great feat. Fire by friction for the first time gave them control over one of the main forces of nature, thereby separating the human race forever from the animal kingdom. "Impressed by the use of fire, primordial humans instituted fire worship when tribes and clans came into existence" (La Fargue 1963:47). In the history of ancient cultures, fire worship was a common phenomenon, and various peoples have kept their customs and tales. Still, however, fire worship in northern China is especially remarkable in its history and extent and in the number of fire deities. Many of the shamanic writings about light and fire in the Far East involve fire worship. Many fire songs, bold and strong and known as fire classics, are wondrous; though buried long in oblivion, they belong to our cultural heritage.

Throughout many centuries, the old fire worship of northern China has been circulating across the area not only because of fire's beauty and light but more importantly because of the warmth it provided in the bitter cold winters. Present archaeology confirms that Siberia was inhabited by humans two hundred thousand to three hundred thousand years ago or even earlier.[11] This suggests that in that primordial era, a branch of human beings went north and occupied that vast region with the help of fire for developing the land. Many historical texts record that the land was all ice and snow, so that "even in summer people had to wear cotton clothes to resist the extreme cold" (Xi Qing 1984). The texts sometimes contain personal testimony: "It is bitterly cold here. . . . Some parts of the land have cracked. Snow turns into hard ice as soon as it falls on the ground. Even direct sunlight cannot melt it away" (Yang Bin et al. 1985). Inhabitants of temperate and hot zones cannot feel the need for fire to the same extent as northern peoples. Fire is like their mother, kind and warm; without it, there is no life. Hence, as we have seen, many shamanic writings and myths, especially of the Manchu, depict fire as a kind-hearted granny, not at all the demonic deity of Han mythology – a three-eyed evil monster with red hair and a green face and body that terrifies people. The fire deity of northern shamanism is personified as the protective deity of all people who dispels cold and evil and brings warmth to all living things. The personification gives expression to a positive view of fire that conveys humankind's great joy over controlling fire.

2.4 Worship of the earth and water

The worship of earth and water has also had a prominent position in northern shamanic nature worship. Some have believed that the worship of the earth and soil came late, but in fact, it was part of the earliest concept of shamanic worship. It was unlike the subsequent worship of Houtu (后土), the god of the earth and soil in Han mythology. It sprang from the primitive understanding that just as heaven has many layers, so too does the earth. Although we can only look far up at the fathomless heavens, we can directly perceive and measure the earth, and by observing caves, tunnels, ravines, springs, cellars, and so on, ancient peoples came to have an awareness that the earth too must be limitless and profound. It gives rise to everything. Our lives can easily be endangered and injured by snakes', pythons', lizards', and insects' crawling up from holes in the ground or by ferocious beasts' suddenly springing out of caves. The earth is thus formidable and mysterious. For primitive human beings, all the sounds and tremors of nature were shrouded in mystery: when the winds blew and cranes cried, when beasts roared, when sounds blasted out from wild jungles, when mountain rocks collapsed on a moonlit or starry night. At the same time, the earth provides all humans and beasts alike with the fruits that they survive on and the places where they dwell. It is thus the base of all things and the source of all life. Beauty and ugliness, excellence and worthlessness, genius and ignorance all spring from it. So ancient human beings regarded it as a god and mother and worshipped it.

In Manchu shamanism, the earth is Banaji Emu (mother earth), Ne Mama, Na Enduri, and Na Khanum. On the basis of the analysis of these terms, we can see that the term of address for earth changed from the feminine mama, to the masculine khanum, which echoes the evolution of shamanism from female deities in early matrilineal clan societies to male gods in patrilineal clans. According to the Manchu shaman Zang,

> Ne Mama was an old woman with black hair and a body full of nipples. What flowed from the nipples was water, and her black hair formed valleys. The sound she made while walking was thunder, and storms arouse when she waved her black hair. When she blew away the sun and moon and changed her hair to white, winter and snow came. The numerous hollows in her flesh were caves in which men and beasts lived and multiplied.

The Manchu creation myth "War in Heaven" tells a similar story:

> Shortly after the birth of the universe, there was a fight between Abka Hehe and the demon Yeluli. Yeluli was originally the black hair in Ne Mama's birch basket, but he was blown into the sky by the Wind Diety Sisilin, and his black hair cast darkness over the universe. He tried to bind up Abka Hehe and prevent the world forever from seeing light. Abka Hehe, however, together with all other beings, waged war against Yeluli, struggling for rule over the universe so as to bring light and warmth to it for good. She had the Hedgehog God to use its spines to entrap Yeluli, and the demon was defeated when his mystic hair lost its magic. He fled back to earth and was buried in itst core by Ne Mama, so that it was pitch dark in the earth's core. Ne Mama had lost quite a few dark hairs, but still had left much white hair. For that reason, there are always more snowy days than warm days on the earth. With her white hair and the storms she arouses when walking, the earth is often visited by ravaging, whirling snowstorms.
>
> (Fu Yuguang and Xing Wenli 2009)

This myth expresses well the perceptions and concepts of northern people.

According to another tale, Mulinmulin Alin (*alin* meaning "mountain") east of the Amur (in Manchu Sahaliyan Ula, Black River) was called Mulinmulin Emu (mother), but the so-called Savage Jurchens of the region called it Cimoni Mama (*cimoni* meaning "breast" in Manchu). Originally, she was a snow mountain goddess whose snow-white skin was always exposed. She lay on her side facing the river while sleeping. When she was sound asleep, the sky was clear; the earth was grassy and permeated with the fragrance of flowers; and melting snow trickled through the mountains, nurturing the earth and animals. When she looked southwards with her eyes open, however, wind and snow would blow up; hail came flooding in; and both humans and animals died. Sahaliyan clanspeople revered her as a shepherd goddess, but later, with the development and reshaping of society, male gods came into ascendancy, and she was transformed into the male god Mulinmulin Khan.

Women's breasts tend to be foregrounded in myths of the earth goddess. Thus, an Ewenki legend has it that "an old woman with huge breasts was credited with the appearance on earth of human beings, who fed on her breast milk and thus were prolific." Many Manchu shamans have believed that if one wants to pay respects to the earth goddess, one must do so on a dark starry night. Fond of stillness, Ne Mama often wanders the earth when all are asleep, visiting her children with milk, fruits, and breaths of fragrance. In the darkness, the mountains, land, rivers, and fields are the shadows of Ne Mama as she sits or sleeps. No one has witnessed her whole body, but she has long hair, and people can make out the hollows in her flesh. Among the star gods, only the eagle star deity has been able to catch sight of Ne Mama's face. For that reason, Ne Mama must be worshipped at night when shamans worship the stars and jangle their girdle bells to summon the help of the wind deity. Her steps can be heard only as they await the wind's visit.

With the development of social productivity, human beings grouped into tribal clans living by mountains and rivers. Each clan cluster had its own representative totem in line with the mountain or river where they dwelt, more often than not one that had an unusual shape. In worshipping mother earth Ne Mama, they regarded mountains as her incarnate representation. Thus, mountain worship came into being. Later, however, in the course of further social development, the image and matriarchal influence of Ne Mama gradually weakened, and the notion of mountain gods' and deities' reflecting particular features of the earth began to grow and solidify into sacrifices offered to a particular mountain, landform, cave, hill, or stone cliff.

The worship of the water god, including that of rivers, lakes, the sea, ice, and snow, has also played an important role in northern shamanism. According to shamanic beliefs in the region, water is inseparable from the earth. The waters of the earth are the breast milk of Ne Mama (Banajiemu), the maternal source of all life. In shamanic mythology, the water god Muke Enduri had its origin in the breast milk of the mother earth, and being born in liquid, this deity takes care of water. The ritual use of water was thus indispensable when worshipping the water god. It must be from clear springs, the depths of the sea, a fresh flowing river, or a well; no stagnant or filthy water should ever be used. Bathing one's eyes and body with clear water, moreover, could exorcise the evil of illness, because clear water is the liquor of the gods.

For her part, the goddess of life Dujin Enduri was born in the sands under the sea. She had eight hands and eight feet, with the depth of the water the same as the length of her feet and her breadth the same as the spread of her hands. Her feet shortened when water became shallow, and when water became less, so did her hands. The goddess had charge of deep waters and resided in the East Sea (Donghai). She was the mother goddess of all life in the sea, and human beings and fish emanated from her every pore. Humans who were brought forth by her on windy days were men. Tossed about by wind and waves, they were thin, and the waves broke out in the form of the male reproductive organs (*coco* in Manchu). Women were born on calm days without waves, so in the past, there were more women than men.

It was also believed in shamanic myths that long ago the earth was flooded, in darkness, and subject to turbulent winds. All was plunged in total darkness. What was born first from the water? Was it *niyalma* (human being)? Was it *nimaha* (fish)? Was it *tasha* (tiger)? Was it *yindahvn* (dog)? No. It was *fodo* (willow); it was the willow deity Moo Enduri. Born in the shape of a *weihū* (canoe), this deity had the shape  and could float on water, run with wind, and reproduce ever more and more abundantly. Eventually, Fodo Moo ("willow" but also "female reproductive organs") came into being. More and more people came to be everywhere because where there was water, there was Fodo Moo. Everything springs from Fodo Moo – flowers, fruits, and human beings. Fodo Moo was born in water, so mother's milk is *muke* (liquid), the *buda* (food) needed to support life. It was believed that the water of the earth gave it its support. If there were no water, the earth would collapse. Similarly, the water in human bodies nurtures human beings, so if the water in one's body gets drained away, one's soul is gone. In shaman myths of the water god, human beings can exist only when there is water. It is the blood and breath of the earth, the source of all things and all life. So water is worshipped with the deepest piety.

According to the Manchu creation myth, when the universe was new, there was a boundless flood, and the waters and heaven were together. In the dark winds, the heavenly mother goddess Abka Hehe made bubbles like tadpoles that reproduced at a fast rate. The more they reproduced, the closer they came together, making a huge ball floating on the waters. Not knowing how much time had passed, six giants jumped out of the ball. They were six *anda* (sworn friends), the ancestors of the Zhushen (Jurchen), and each had charge of one direction – east, west, south, north, up, or down. Together they had thirty-six eyes, a pair on each one's head, hands, and feet, so they could see everything. They had forty-eight feet, so they could walk fast and could go everywhere. They had forty-eight hands, so everything was within their reach.

Northern peoples have also traditionally deified water snakes, called water dragons (*shuilong*), and their spirit idols have the shape of snakes, big fish, otters, or the scorpion or lizard god with four legs. A myth recounts how the water dragon goddess Mukemuduri Enduri was exalted by the Jurchen to the position of one of the most ancient gods of the universe. Her armpit hair turned into numerous Mukemuduri (water dragons) that swallowed up the water day and night when Abka Hehe waged war against Yeluli after he flooded the earth. The more they swallowed, the heavier they became, and in the end, they could not move but rather turned into numerous long, wide, sparkling *charhan* (small rivers). White rivers swallowed white water and stones; black rivers swallowed black water and stones. They lay still on the earth and became huge long streams from a distant source. There was too much water in the bellies of these giant dragons, so some became fountains. Others were hemmed in by the huge flood, so they wriggled their way through the earth and fled. They gorged up a long ditch and finally found the East Sea, guided by the chirping of birds. Magpies and crows call all day because they are helping send all the dragon gods to find pools of water and the sea.

Because of their fondness for and beliefs about water, northern peoples have had some special folk customs. They have commonly lived at the foot of a hill beside a stream, and "there was no social decorum in ancient northern customs, in the sense that the ruler bathed in the same streams and walked along the same paths as ordinary citizens" (Hong Hao 1868). Their customs were simple and unconstrained by propriety. High and low alike, they all believed that washing in streams can bring them good fortune and rid them of contagious diseases. They worshipped small water mammals and reptiles as mascots and fetishes, so frogs, snakes, lizards, waterfowls, and so on frequently appear on shaman drums, costumes, and spirit idols.

In the past, northern peoples who lived alongside rivers had the custom of water burial. They used stones or sand to sink the corpse of a deceased shaman deep in the water and sent it downstream into the sea, ushering their soul back to the origin of life – water. The entry "Heilongjiang" in the Chinese *Social Life and Customs* recounts that "it was customary to use cremation or water burial, sinkng the corpse in the high tide" (Hu Pu'an 1986). When shamans of the Manchu, Hezhe, Xibe, and other northern peoples made glutinous rice cakes to offer to the gods, they would beat their drums to enliven the rice and sprinkle water. Some Manchu clans have sacred songs about water, such as "The mother's rain began to fall, and the places where clans live, inner and outer, were all drenched with rain. Coming with the rain were the gods, and gone with it were evil spirits."

Finally, the ice god and snow god are related to the invincible sacred power of wind and water. Some shamanic myths say that ice and snow were made by the evil god Yeluli. When fighting with Abka Hehe, he cast stones of wind to quench stones of fire, so the northern sky became frigid. He gave Abka Hehe a wily challenge. He asked her what the most beautiful thing in the world is, and she answered that it is the colour white. For her, the universe was golden white, and the earth's rivers rushed with white water. She did not know that Yeluli had stolen Banajiemu's white hair and covered the world with never-melting snow and thick ice. The snow and ice piled up like snow-capped mountains, and all creatures died. When Abka Hehe realized the truth, it was too late. The universe had turned into a white snow-covered world of freezing cold. She made the sun and stars shine and made the winds howl, but the ice and snow were too thick to melt. For this reason, it takes a long time for snowy days to warm up. An Oroqen legend has it that the wind goddess Feng Popo (风婆婆) took the ice and snow with her as she was wandering about in her wind carriage, mistaking them for clouds. That is why snow keeps falling and the sound of her wind carriage can be heard when it snows.

On the whole, the worship of water in northern shamanism is not as prevalent as that of fire, and the sacred chants and rituals honouring water are inferior to those for honouring fire. The reason for this may be that the freezing cold of the

North lasts five to six months of the year, so northern ancestors worshipped the warming fire god as the most important deity.

2.5 Worship of sacred birds

Many scholars in China and beyond are interested in the reverence of crows among the Manchu. Ever since the era of the Republic of China (1912–1949), numerous works have cited ancient bird worship as a part of the cultural history and primitive mythology of the Manchu and other northern peoples of China, Siberia, and Northeast Asia. Many peoples had the concept that sacred birds favour their world, and they developed many unique living habits, interests, and taboos related to birds in the long process of social development. Among Manchu customs, worshipping the magpie is well known, the earliest record of which can be found in documents of the Qing dynasty. *Veritable Records of the Qing Emperor Nurhaci* (*Qingzaizu nu'erhachi shilu*) recounts that a red fruit in a divine magpie's mouth was swallowed by Fogulun, a celestial nymph from Yuan Lake of the Changbai Mountains, and she became pregnant. She gave birth to Bukūri Yongšon, who "named his clan Manchu and became the primogenitor of the Manchu" (*Qingtaizu nupanyachi shilu* 1989). This creation myth has been told from generation to generation and refers to the origin of the Aisin Gioro Hala, the imperial clan of Manchu emperors from present-day Yilan (*aisin* meaning "gold"). Another Aisin Gioro magpie myth is documented in *Veritable Records of the Manchu* (*Manzhou shilu*), the most authoritative Qing record of magpie mythology:

> Several of Bukūri Yongšon's descendants of the Odoli family were tyrannical, and their subordinates rebelled. In June, the Odoli were raided; and all clan descendants were killed except the boy Fanca, who fled into the wilderness. As he was being pursued by the foe, a sacred magpie perched on his head. The enemy thought there was no way that magpies could perch on a person's head, so they mistook the child for dead wood and went away. Fanca was thus saved and hid out until his death. All Manchu descendants regard magpies as divine and never do them harm.
>
> (*Manzhou shilu* 1986)

Before Qing Emperor Huang Taiji (1592–1643) changed the name of his people from Jurchen to Manchu, there were widespread Jurchen myths of about divine magpies soaring in the heavens and saving creatures caught in floodwaters. In the flood myth The Celestial Princess Bai Yun (*Baiyun gege*), Bai Yun, the third daughter of the god of heaven, was greatly pleased with magpies who cast green twigs about so that all the creatures on earth were saved from the flood and multiplied. In "War in Heaven," a sacred magpie was the maid of the heavenly mother Abka Hehe. To defeat the devil Yeluli, Abka Hehe wanted to eat pebbles from the East Sea to gain strength, so the magpie flew about to pick up stones every day and carry them back in its mouth. Tired on the way back, it perched on a sacred tree to rest. The magpie was revered for this feat, and in Manchu tradition, the tree stretching up to the sky has also been celebrated, not only because of its great height but also because it was the perch of the sacred magpie.

Like the Inuit, who worshipped crows and forbade killing them, the Manchu also worshipped crows with great devotion and honoured them in the shamanic pantheon. In fact, as can be confirmed from handwritten oracles of some Manchu clans, crow worship far outweighed that of the magpie among the Manchu and other northern peoples and is even more ancient and widespread. Injuring or capturing crows was strictly prohibited, and they were worshipped in Manchu rituals that used a newly cut pole as a symbol of contact with the spirit realm above. *The Collected Records of Jilin* (*Jilin huizheng*) recounts that "the Manchu used sacrificial poles in the courtyard. They put pig intestines and lungs in a bowl and placed it on top of the pole to worship crows" (Xileng Guo 1914). Some Manchu clans regarded crows as their ancestors:

> They would set up a pole in the center of the courtyard and at the top tie a cloth symbolizing the ancestors. They then slaughtered a pig and chopped up its meat. When a flock of birds descended and ate it all up, people would say that the ancestors are satisfied and rejoice. If the meat was not eaten, people would be anxious and say that the ancestors were frightened or angered and that disaster was approaching.
>
> (Ning'an Annals Editorial Committee 1989)

In a Manchu household in Gongzhuling, Jilin Province, there was a bird-shaped spirit idol to the left of a sacred box for shamanic paraphernalia on the west *kang* (heatable raised bed platform). It was said by clanspeople that the idol was a crow god who rescued the chieftain Nurhaci. In the belief of the Negidal people who inhabited the lower reaches of the Amur and had an influence on ancient Manchu culture, crows used to be human beings. This accords with what is said in the rites of the Husihali Hala of Ning'an, Heilongjiang, that "the crow is a princess guarding the woods" as goddess of the forests.

The Oroqen believed that cawing forest crows were mourning something bad that would happen. If you heard them calling overhead on the way, there was bound to be a misfortune, accident, or the death of a horse. So everyone acted with extreme caution and were convinced that crows have an ability of divination. The Feiyaka (Nivkh) of China and formerly Russia held the belief that crows were sent to the earth by the supreme god of heaven. They thus venerated them as high gods and assumed that they had existed ever since the creation of the universe. Manchu ancestors and other northern hunters would sprinkle liquor and meat for them when they offered a sacrifice to the forest.

Crows have other mythic associations. The Qiahela and Manchu Nimaca and Namdulu Hala dwelling in the wild forests of the Ussuri River sometimes brought into their villages giant pythons which were accidentally found in the forests. Called *jabjan* in the Manchu language, the python was considered the messenger of the sun. Its colourful skin pattern was thought to be the incarnation of a rainbow, and its flaming red tongue the incarnation of fire. To invite the sacred python to descend to earth, adults and children would imitate crows' "caw, caw, caw" and dance with joy, hoping that the python would bring light and warmth to the world.

As is recorded in the Manchu epic *Umesiben Mama*, the crow used to be a diligent attendant of the god of heaven Abka Enduri, but it was starving in wartime and mistakenly ate the poisonous plant *heicao* (black grass) and died. Later, it turned into a bird with black feathers and harsh cries circling around mountain villages. Fond as they are of pecking at the remains of animals and human beings, crows were believed to be the wolves of heaven. In shamanic lore, moreover, their black colour is the colour of dead souls and the skin of the evil god Yeluli. Thee Manchu hold the colour white in high esteem, but have traditionally been frightened by what is black. Crow reverence reflects this fear. At the same time, however, shaman lore has it that because crows' feathers are of a dark, sunless colour, they can warn humans and animals of danger. On suddenly spying ill omens or animal carcasses in the woods or wilderness, they caw in the sky to let humans know. *Veritable Records of the Manchu* mentions that when the founder of the Qing dynasty, Nurhaci, fought against Ming soldiers, a flock of crows blocked the enemy and acquainted Nurhaci with the military situation (*Manzhou shilu* 1986). Although he was greatly outnumbered, he was thus able to completely defeat the attackers and increase his power.

The respect for the breeding of crows had grown into a general trend in the Qing dynasty:

> In the open space west of the Imperial Palace at Shengjing (盛京, present-day Shenyang), grains were scattered to feed crows. They would then flock together, hovering, perching, pecking at the food, preening themselves, flapping their wings, and cawing. Millions of them occupied almost the whole roof of the Imperial Palace.
>
> (Xu Ke 1984)

People from various Manchu clans valued crows and did no harm to them. The flocks of crows scattering throughout clan settlements were taken as a sign that the clans would thrive and be affluent. Both crows and magpies are indigenous to northern China. Crows had a high place first and foremost in peoples' consciousness. In contrast, magpies were venerated for another reason: they cause no harm to human beings and animals, and with their white necks and bellies, their slender beauty elevated them to the status of maids of the celestial gods in folktales. Because both types of fowl were greatly venerated, moreover, in the classic literature of the Qing dynasty, their influence and status became even more heightened.

The reverence of birds was by no means limited to magpies and crows; nor did it first flourish in the Qing dynasty. Northern forefathers regarded birds as a symbol of sanctity and good fortune, as can be seen from both modern archaeological discoveries and historical documents. Unearthed cultural artefacts reveal that the worship of birds in the North existed as early as Neolithic Age. Russian archaeologists have found numerous images of goddesses and birds carved in rock in the Amur River basin. *Relics of Baicheng* (*Baicheng yizhi*) notes that among the unearthed artefacts, there was a sculpted relief, polished on one side with two birds on the other. In 1955, Russian scholars found bricks with bird patterns in the Tucheng of the Jin dynasty (1115–1234) along the Ussuri River. Chinese archaeologists found a precious hawk head exquisitely caved out of bone and shaped like a quarter moon in Mishan, Heilongjiang. It is consistent with the hawk-shaped spirit idols with a human body and bird wings worshipped by Manchu shamans. Numerous bones of birds, fish, and beasts and fragments of clam shells in a primitive site in Lishu, Jilin Province, have also been unearthed, as have bone beads in the shape of slim tubes from the limbs of birds in the ancient tombs at Kalunshan, Heihe City, Heilongjiang (Li Jiancai 1986:69). Such artefacts are too many to enumerate. They mirror the interests and superb artistic skills of ancient ancestors while giving evidence of their bird worship.

Ancient Chinese documents also give evidence of bird worship. It is reported in *Book of Jin* (*Jin Shu*), the official account of the early Jin dynasty (265–420 CE) that was compiled in 648, that the Sushen, the ancient forebearers of the Manchu,

> (also called Yilou) lived in the north of Buxian Shan (Changbai Shan).[12] A man would stick feathers in a woman's hair, and if the woman accepted him, he would ask her to be his wife and marry her in a formal, respectful way.
>
> (Fang Xuanling 1974)

This custom of regarding bird feathers as a pledge of love was passed down into the Yuan and Ming dynasties. Feathers were also used in headdresses: "The Heishui Mohe[13] (ancestors of the Jurchen, who were in turn ancestors of the Manchu) had the custom of using wild boar tusks and a pheasant's tail feathers for their headdress" (Fan Ye 1965). A similar account can be found in *Collected Records of Jilin*: "It was a custom among the Heishui Mohe to use the pheasant's tail feather as headdress, and Russian women in modern times followed suit." *Records of the Great Jin* (*Dajin guozhi*) notes that the later Jin dynasty (1115–1234), founded by the Wanyan clan of the Heishui (Black River) Mohe, used the sun, the moon, and the falcon as embroidered patterns on their campaign banners, from which we know about their worship of sacred birds. *Travels of East Tartary* (*Dongda jixing*)[14] recounts that bird patterns were used as well on the masts of official ships of the area as a safety charm.

Throughout Liao, Jin, and early Qing days, the Jurchen retained their traditional habit of wearing feather caps and coats, weaving feather curtains, and using feather bedding, and rich people used feathers to cover their roofs. Young Jurchen girls wore a tube-shaped, five-coloured beading with ornamental engraving made of bird-neck bones. The beading made a tuneful, sonorous sound and was considered a talisman against evil spirits. According to the recollection of Manchu elders, when girls got married during the period of the Republic of China, the Manchu of Ning'an and some other regions made capes with beautiful buckwheat, leopard-spot, or cat's-eye patterns woven from pheasant plumes. After the wedding, the cape would be treasured and worn only for New Year visits or festivals. For some Manchu newlyweds, after the *baitiandi* (拜天地, their worship of heaven and earth during a wedding) and the *zuozhang* (坐□, the bride's sitting on the marriage bed or *kang* for good fortune and happiness), her mother would change the bride's hair style from *liangbatou* to *yibazhua*, sticking clumps of brightly coloured plumes with a beautiful decorative pattern that had an auspicious meaning.

In some areas, swan feathers were often used at weddings. Legend has it that swans and other waterfowl were maids of mother earth Banaji Emu, who had charge of the earth's waters. So swans were regarded as sacred birds by the ancestors of the Manchu and some other northern peoples. According to legend, there was a river named Swan River in the upper reaches of the Sungari. Since sacred swans can foretell floods and droughts as they honk in flight, the river was named after them. The Hezhe presented swans as sacrificial offerings to their gods, and Manchu swan sacrifice is documented in *Introduction to the Annals of Changbai Mountain* (*Changbaishan huigang zhilue*). Using images of swans and other birds for divination and exorcism was a universal practice among northern peoples (Li Shutian 1987). The Manchu, Xibe, Hezhe, and Oroqen used bird patterns, moreover, for house decorations as good luck charms. When building a new house, the Ewenki (Goldi) in Russia would put cigarette butts and smashed bowls under two wooden house pillars and corner pillars, to prevent evil spirits from coming in and to ward off hunger, and would tie to the house beam a strand of eagle feathers, along with a strip of red cloth and a small packet of millet. It was said that eagle feathers could ensure that the house would be solid and the owner safe and sound.

Regarded as both spirits and intimate friends, sparrows and other small birds have been favoured as well by northern peoples. When sparrows flutter around silently, the house is without mishap, but when they get raucous, there is danger of fire, poisonous snakes, or pestilence just around the corner. Sparrows are smart by nature, frightened of fire and smoke, and perceptive of the slightest things. For that reason, people have deemed them sacred birds. Huozhuor, a female deity worshipped by the Daur, is said to have become a golden sparrow after death: "She swam gaily as a carp and became a companion of wild goldfish" (Inner Mongolia Editorial Committee 1986b:52). The Niaomai goddess of the Ewenki, Kazak, Uygur, and Kirgiz in China, as well as the Nanai, Ewenki, Negidal, Buryat, Kachin, and Khakas of Russia, was a little sparrow in charge of infants and subsequently revered as the goddess protector of infants. Sparrows made of birch or larch have traditionally been worshipped among the Ewenki in the hope that they would protect infants from danger. The same notion has been shared by the Manchu and Hezhe. They believe that chirping sparrows are like lively children and are incarnations of the souls of *tongzi* (童子, a child younger than fourteen). When retrieving the soul of a child, if a sparrow was seen flying past, people believed that the soul had returned. The child would recover, disaster would vanish, and the whole family would rejoice. Many clans put sparrow-shaped spirit idols on their altars.

Some Manchu clans worshipped the seedling god on hearing cuckoos in spring and the snow mama on seeing finches in winter. As legend goes, the finch was a girl who went to a snow-capped mountain north of the Siyanggun Bira (river) to hunt eagles with her father and died in a snow avalanche. She would subsequently go down south every year to seek out her family and was idolized by Jurchens.

Bird worship has occupied an important place in northern shamanic ritual costumes and mimic gestures for summoning or sending off gods. Bird deities vary depending on clan location. There were traditionally from two or three to five or seven such deities for every clan, including waterfowl like ducks, geese, and swans; predatory birds like eagles, vultures, and falcons; and pigeons and doves – covering every possible bird species. The eagle and vulture gods were particularly respected and worshipped because of their invincible might. According to the shaman schema of the Nine Realms of the Heavens (*Cangqiong jiutian*, 苍穹九天), all gods reside in the far-off lofty shrines of golden mansions in the firmament. They descend to earth by the light of the Big Dipper when summoned by ritual drumbeats, but in the minds of primordial humans, their majestic mansions were far beyond the reach of earthly beings. Only birds, with their magical wings, could soar into the heavens, so they had an aura of supernatural mystery. As the messengers of heaven and incarnations of gods or spirits, they could travel freely between heaven and earth, between the gods and human beings. They were thought to possess the power of the nature deities – fire, light, wind, thunder, rain, hail, and so on – and to be as powerful and invincible as animal deities. Hence in the trance dance of *ye* rituals (*yeji*, 野祭), shamans would summon bird deities by mimicking the flight of birds in a dynamic and bustling, but reverent, moving atmosphere.

Bird ornaments have been the most common fetish on shaman costumes, such as the fluttering bird ornaments on Manchu headdresses and a perching bird on those of the Udege. According to *The Guidebook of Ethnic Plastic Arts in the Amur River Basin* (*Heilongjiang liuyu minzu zaoxing yishu shouce*) by Russian scholar C.B. Ivanov, the Oroch people in Russia believed that when a shaman's soul goes to the sun, it first rides a white horse, then a ball of yarn, then a bird, and finally an iron boat with wings. The Udege would sew four strands of eagle feathers on the back, shoulders, and sleeves of their shaman gowns and let three long fabric ribbons fall down their backs from the collar. The Orochi had the same costume, with feathers on the shoulder blades (Ivanov 1990). The Daur had cuckoo spirit idols carved out of old willow wood enshrined in shamans' homes. Xibe shamans included the eagle god and other bird gods and the deer god in their pantheon, and they worship the eagle with various ritual gestures. The traditional Hezhe name of the eagle goddess is Kori, and the Oroqen portray Deleku Daryir, the deity of convulsions, on a sacred cloth together with two fierce birds, two dragons, two pythons, and a sun and moon. The Ewenki peel off the skin of at bird to fashion a flying horse named *Sewenki*. Their shamans believed that spirit idols made from bird skin could fly freely. They used idols made from the skin of two woodpeckers when praying for rain. They would put the woodpeckers inside a vessel full of water with their beaks facing upwards and hang them on branches, hoping that they could thus achieve their goal by bird magic (Qiu Pu

1962). Russian scholars relate that Siberian Ewenki worshipped a dozen kinds of bird idols, including the Niaomai bird god and especially the teal god. Their creation myth speaks of human beings made of bird feathers and bird flesh.

From these various categories of bird gods, we can see that primordial human beings formed an indissoluble bond with waterfowls for their fishing and hunting livelihood. Whenever northern ancestors held a sacrificial rite, they first made offerings to waterfowl deities – swan, cormorant, white water birds, and so on. When the gods descended, shamans would perform a bird dance and bird walk, all the while drumming, jangling their waist bells, and whirling the copper sparrow and long ribbons on their headdresses. The dance symbolized the sacred bird's flight – now whirling, now diving to catch fish, now soaring into sky – always followed by the assistant *zaili*. The solemn yet passionate bird dance was not just a simple imitative gesture; it often demonstrated the extraordinary origin and particular function of the bird deity being worshipped. Some Manchu clans have had as their totem the white water bird goddess in charge of floods, who brings rain and flying stones as she descends. According to legend, she was transformed from a white maiden. Long ago, when the earth was deluged with raging waves, a caring shamaness caught fish for her clanspeople to satisfy their hunger. She was a good swimmer and could swim hundreds of kilometres. Once, however, she mistook a white fish in the water for a stone and dashed it against a rock. The fish died, and after the shaman's own death, *shei* became incarnated as a sacred bird with white feathers. The bird had the divine power of swallowing water and moving stones, and its cries could forecast weather and floods.

Some forest birds have enjoyed the same ritual status as waterfowls. Such are Weji Gasha (forest bird god), Alin Gasha (mountain bird god), the supreme eagle Dala Giyahvn, the supreme vulture Dala Damin, and other eagle deities. Along with the vulture, the eagle god symbolizes power and light as the most ferocious divinity of the universe. The god has two silver claws resting on its breast and golden wings which can cover earth and snow. Ruling the earth's light and darkness, it bears the sun in the daytime and drives it away at night. Eagle gods have had great significance in shamanic rituals, traditionally appearing as a figure on shaman costumes and celebrated in sacred texts. Manchu texts recount that the earth was just a clump of ice when the universe was born. Abka Hehe dispatched a female eagle to fly past the sun while fluffing out her feathers to load light and fire and then fly to earth. From then on, the earth's ice and snow melted at times, so that human beings and all living creatures could have food and rest and breed. However, the eagle was so tired that she once nodded off to sleep, and the fire in her feathers fell down, setting the forest and stones on fire, which burnt day and night. She put out the flames with her huge wings and used her claws to dig up dirt to smother the flames. However, she died in the sea of raging flames, and her soul was transformed into a shamaness. So a shamaness's soul is an indomitable eagle. There are also two Russian bird tales about the origin of shamans. According to one, the first shaman was the guide eagle Di; according to the other, the eagle taught human beings how to perform the trance dance. In both legends, the eagle has two heads, but ever since it taught people how to perform the dance, it lost one of its heads.

Because of their divine power and blood relationship with shamans, the eagle god and vulture god became the patrons and incarnations of shamans. According to shaman texts of the Seven Manchu Donghai (East Sea) Clans, during the era of the flood, a little seal rescued a man and woman, who then gave birth to a baby girl. Abka Hehe ordered the eagle-headed, female-bodied princess goddess to raise the baby, who subsequently became the first female master shaman. In a similar Mongol Buryat legend, the eagle god sent a vulture down to help human beings, and the first shaman was born by the vulture and a Buryat woman. The Yakuts also believed that shamans are descendants of the eagle.

The eagle god not only represents celestial light but also possesses the gift of roaming the world. It can visit the underworld, spreading out light and heat, and exorcise ghosts and monsters. The heroine of the famous Manchu folk epic "Nishan Shaman" was the shamaness Yin Jiang, who visited the underworld to rescue the souls of two children under the guidance of the eagle god. There she contended with the Manchu lord of the underworld Ilmun Khan and, assisted by the eagle god, brought them back to earth.

The religious concept of bird worship is revealed mainly in many primitive creation myths. In "War in Heaven," the myth of the Jurchen group called Savage Jurchen by the Han Chinese of the Ming dynasty, the following is told of a sacred bird:

> At the birth of the universe, there was no sun, moon, stars, or any other celestial body. Everything was plunged in darkness. Abka Hehe and Yeluli made a bet on who could be powerful enough to find light and see the color of the sky and earth. With his devil eyes, Yeluli found white ice among masses of ice in the darkness. He moved an ice-capped mountain to illuminate the universe, but it turned out that everything was frozen. At her wit's end, Abka Hehe was borne up to the sky by a celestial bird who pecked a hole in the sky, then another, and finally thousands of holes in the sky. From then on, the sun, moon, and stars appeared, and there was light and warmth, so that the ice and snow brought by Yeluli continuously melted.
>
> (Fu Yuguang and Jing Wenli 2009)

From this myth, we can see that Manchu ancestors regarded birds as spirits that appeared together with the formation of the earth and the appearance of fire. In ancient times among northern peoples, there must have been a relationship between the discovery of fire and the activity of birds. People thus associated birds with fire and the sun and expressed this relationship in fantastic myths.

"War in Heaven" also speaks of the role of a sacred bird in the fight between Abka Hehe and Yeluli:

> Yeluli tore up the battle suit of Abka Hehe, and she was injured and fell down by Sun River. There was a sacred tree in the river, with a golden sparrow

> perching on its branches. It took pity on the injured Abka Hehe and gathered water from the river to wash her wounds and wiped her wounds with its colorful feathers. Abka Hehe soon came to her senses, and with her limitless power restored, defeated the devil Yeluli and acquired dominion over the universe.
>
> (Fu Yuguang and Jing Wenli 2009)

The invincible might of the sparrow could thus protect even the god Abka Hehe, which shows that Manchu ancestors worshipped the bird god with great veneration.

The Ancient Cultures of Siberia (*Xiboliya de gudai wenhua*) recalls the role that a sacred bird had in the myth of three suns preserved among peoples in the Amur basin:

> At the very beginning of the earth, there were three suns in the sky, scorching the earth and melting stones. A hero named Huotai appeared and shot two of the suns down, so that the earth became warm and pleasant. When the sky was on fire, a bird was the first to step on the melted stones, leaving its claw prints. Therefore, it was considered a deity contemporary with the beginning of the universe.
>
> (Jilin Archaeological Research Office 1975)

According to another myth, the kindly deities who first created the earth in the time of the flood and thus made it possible for humankind to live and multiply were not anthropomorphic gods but gods who had the image of birds. They were white water birds whose colour was the same as the waves and white-feathered swans who were good at diving and picking out sand and stones. At the origin of the universe, there was flood water everywhere and no dwelling place for land creatures. White water birds, with the help of wild ducks, wild geese, wild swans, and so on, fetched sand and stones to make beach lands. In this way, the earth was formed. A similar myth has been widely spread among northern peoples, but it need not be given here.

On the whole, northern peoples shared many common shamanic myths and customs regarding divine birds that created the world and were the primogenitors of human beings. With the passage of time and the vicissitudes of ethnic migrations, the myths and corresponding customs came to have numerous variations. Research studies on bird deities have offered new insights into the treasure hoard of these myths, their religious ideology, and peoples' corresponding folk customs. Northern peoples' cultural consciousness was formed in the process of contact with the natural living conditions of northeastern China, Siberia, and Far East Asia, which are home to one of the largest bird habitats in the world. People lived in the wilderness of the Changbai Mountain, the Amur River, and the East Sea, and modern scientific expeditions have confirmed that the vast expanse of land marked out by the Yellow Sea in the south, the Sea of Okhotsk in the north, and the East Sea (Sea of Japan) in the east has long been a paradise for bird breeding.

There are numerous islands, lakes, and rivers near the estuary of the Amur that constitute an ideal breeding place for all kinds of fish and shrimp because of the long sunlight in summer and moisture in spring and autumn. With its plentiful supply of food and ideal conditions for breeding and habitation, the whole area is an ideal home for a variety of indigenous and migrant wildfowl. The ancestors of today's northern peoples lived, multiplied, and developed together with the birds in this fertile bird kingdom.

Northern bird folktales include "Bird Guiding to Treasure," "Crossing the Sea on Goose Feathers," "Marrying the Bird Maiden," "The Bird God Rescuing Humans from the Flood," and many others. During primeval times when productivity was underdeveloped, birds did not contribute much to humans in terms of food and clothing, but birds were humans' companions in life. One Manchu tale tells of a hero who went into the mountains to look for his wife, a deer, and got lost in the forest. With the help of a woodpecker, he climbed to the top of the sacred mountain and found her, the beautiful deer princess, who had been hidden in a hollow tree by a demon. People could predict misfortune and abnormal phenomena by birds' frightened cries and flight directions, and they built their houses and caves on the basis of the shapes and principles of bird nests. Owing to their contribution to humankind, the bird gods were generally worshipped as gentle and kind protective clan deities.

In primordial times when productivity was underdeveloped, we can imagine that once fire was discovered, some groups began to move north in search of better means of survival. They must have found it hard, however, to find their way in the wild forests, and as is said in a shamanic text, there were fog-bound lakes and swamplands with clumps of grass everywhere. To survive, they would have needed to observed the movements of migrant birds and so tracked their northbound route. We can see traces of this in shamanic rituals. When shamans summon bird deities, the shamans walk like birds in the *bazi* gait with toes pointing outwards, the *guaizi* gait with feet cast sideways, and the *suolian* gait with progressive cross-steps. Their *zaili* assistants and clanspeople follow in step, singing, chanting, and dancing joyfully. The ancient Manchus believed, moreover, that if a hunter could find white bird droppings in the forest, the hunter could follow such markings as signposts and "sparrow's calligraphy," given to humankind so that we would not get lost. In the battle between Abka Hehe and Yeluli in *Umesiben Mama*, and the shamanic tale *Sirin Sefu*, Abka Hehe got lost but finally found a way to attack Yeluli with the help of bird droppings on forest trees. In primitive matriarchal clan society, there thus must have been clans whose totems were birds. With the passage of time, however, only totems of magpies, crows, and some water birds can be found.

Notes

1 This classic Mongolian literary work was written for the Mongol royal family sometime after Genghis Khan's death in 1227 CE, by an anonymous author. It was probably originally in the Uygur script, though the surviving texts all derive from a Ming

dynasty transcription into Chinese at the end of the 14th century under the name *The Secret History of the Yuan Dynasty.* It is regarded as the single most significant native Mongol account of Genghis Khan.

2 This was recorded in an unpublished shamanic text of the Manchu Hu 胡clan, Hunchun County 珲春县, Jilin Province.

3 The Xibe were a Tungus people living mostly near North Korea in Xinjiang, Jilin, and Liaoning.

4 *History of Yuan (Yuan shi*元史) is one of the official history works in *Twenty-Four Histories of China*, commissioned by the Ming dynasty (1368–1844) and composed in 1370 under the direction of Song Lian 宋濂.

5 Möngke Khan (1209–1259) was the fourth great khan of the Mongol Empire and the first of the Toluid line. He made significant reforms to improve the administration of the empire; and under him, the Mongols conquered Iraq, Syria, and the kingdom of Nanzhao.

6 History of Liao (Liáo shǐ 辽史) was commissioned by the Yuan dynasty (1271–1368) under the direction of the Mongol historian Toqtoya (Tuotuo 脱脱) and finalized in 1344.

7 History of Jin (*Jinshi* 金史) was the official dynastic history of the Jurchen Great Jin dynasty (1115–1234), compiled during the Yuan period under the supervision of Toqtoya.

8 The Seven Hulun Clans were Husihali Hala, Namdulu Hala, Nimaca Hala, Hexeri Hala, Cigujila Hala, Sumri Hala, and Niohuru Hala.

9 The Sushen were the ancestors of the Mohe, Jurchen, Manchu, and other Tungusic peoples. They lived in caves and trees in the north of China, used flint-headed arrows, and farmed, hunted, and fished.

10 *Yimakan* 伊玛堪 is the traditional Hezhe folk chant or recitative (Chinese general term *shuochang*说唱) that reflects their ancient history, means of livelihood, life and customs and is called a living fossil or encyclopaedia of Hezhe culture.

11 See news report about a Russian scholar's archaeological discoveries in Xinhua Press, May 14, 1985.

12 Changbai Shan长白山 (Ever White Mountain), first recorded in the *Classic of Mountains and Seas* (Shanhaijin《山海经》) under the name Buxian Shan 不咸山.

13 Heishui Mohe 黑水靺鞨, Heuksu Malgal, or Black-River Mohe were the most feared among the Mohe tribes. They lived along the Amur (Heilongjiang, Black Dragon River), in the Manchu language Sahaliyan Ula (Black River) in Inner Mongolia.

14 East Tartary was old name for the Manchu-inhabited territory from the confluence of the Amur and Ussuri rivers at Khabarovsk to Sakhalin Island.

3 Ancestor and fertility worship

Ancestor worship is an important aspect of northern polytheist shamanism, and numerous scholarly works in China and beyond touch on this topic. Ancestor worship evolved from other forms of worship, such as the nature and totem worship of matriarchal clan society, and it amounts to a higher level of ancient religious worship. It came into prominence with human social development when marital unions had become monogamous or polygamous and men came to have the dominant position in patriarchal society. As the power of male chieftains and family heads was growing, social mores came to centre on paternity; patriarchy became the code of social life; and the worship of natural forces evolved into the worship of one's male ancestors.

3.1 Ancestor worship

Ancestor worship focuses mainly on the worship of the souls and spirit idols of ancestors of the male bloodline. It was believed that their souls are immortal and inhabit a world of light in the sacred mansions of the nine heavens, where they enjoy the same life as earthlings but one more comfortable and joyful. It was believed, moreover, that their noble souls were endowed with such invincible power and supernatural ability that they could freely roam the expanse of the universe and visit their descendants on earth, whom they protected and blessed as guardian deities in a caring and familiar manner. The ancestral deities of northern shamanism served as an emotional bond among clans, neighbouring clans, *mukūn* (paternal subclan, a Jurchen legacy), villages, and families in patriarchal society and provided a strong sense of communal cohesion.

As is the case with the ancestral rites of peoples all over the world, the shamanic ancestor worship of northern peoples originally focused on the ancestors of a particular clan or group, but it subsequently developed into the worship of the common ancestors of allied clans or tribes. Later, as family units grew up one after another, ancestor worship within the family came to pass. One feature shared among these three forms of ancestor worship is that they all regard the spirits of their own bloodline ancestors as sacred spirits and deities, while those of other clans are regarded as extraneous and even harmful ghosts. Therefore, northern ancestor worship is to some extent exclusive. People acknowledge only the patriarchal spirits within the same clan or tribe as their protective deities and do not worship those of other clans. It was believed that other ancestral spirits do not protect and bless their offspring but rather are evil spirits to be avoided and exorcised. In the case of exogamous marriage, however, the ancestral spirits of the bride's clan could be brought into the husband's family.

The clan ancestors worshipped in northern shamanism include the following:

> The primogenital patriarchal deity of the clan; pioneer and hero deities; heroic martyrs of clan expeditions; spirits of first-generation clan shamans and ancient hereditary shamans; spirits of deceased ancestors registered in clan genealogies. The deities worshipped in the Qing court were also ancestor deities.

The majority of ancestral deities have traditionally been male, but many female clan deities have also been worshipped, especially among the Manchu, which have numerous maternal goddesses. The far-reaching influence of maternal goddesses in ancient northern matriarchal clans continues to hold a strong inspirational force. When matriarchal society was flourishing, female shamans were regarded as a kind of protective goddess of the clan, and they continued to hold a powerful position after clan society became patriarchal. In fact, most shamans of the patriarchal clans of the Manchu and other northern ethnic minorities, such as the Oroqen, Xibe, Hezhe, Daur, and various Siberian and East Asian peoples have been female, even in powerful feudal society. After the founding of the People's Republic of China in 1949, among the Manchu clans of Yongji in Jilin Province and Ning'an in Heilongjiang, female shamans have had absolute superiority in presiding over shamanic rituals as the hereditary shaman of the clan.

The three forms of shamanic ancestor worship mentioned earlier – ancestors of a particular clan, common ancestors of allied clans, and ancestors of a particular family – have found expression in various ways. In the most ancient times, they found concrete expression among northern peoples as human-beast deities or deities concretized as physical objects. Among the former are the eagle-headed, woman-bodied or the woman-headed, leopard-bodied spirit effigies preserved in the sacred repositories of some Manchu clans. Among the latter are birch bark figures in the shape of a willow leaf standing for the female pudendum and stone or clay figures in the shape of male genitalia.

Some clans lost track of their original ancestral fetishes, due to long-time migration and assimilation with other clans, but they preserved some typical objects of worship from their ancestors. For example, the Manchu Xu clan originally lived along the Zeya River (in Manchu Jingkiri Bira; in Chinese Jingqili River), a northern tributary of the Amur, but they subsequently migrated to the Sungari (Songhua) basin, where they still worship three pebbles from the Zeya River, just as their ancestors did. They do so in their clan *jia* rituals (*jiaji*, 家祭),[1] shaman rites influenced by Qing court rites and standardized in the mid-Qing era without spirit possession and not necessarily a family rite, though *jia* basically means "house" or "home." Other objects enshrined as spirit fetishes among northern peoples include a piece of leather or wood, pottery fragments, a birch or straw basket, fur, a bird feather, fish bone, stone needle, or stone arrowhead passed down from ancestors.

An interesting legend says that the Oroqen invited the ancestors of the Daur into their homes, worshipped them, and sacrificed fresh meat to them every day, which indicates that the ancestor worship of these two peoples originated from similar or related tribes. The same is true for some Manchu clans, in which one clan would take into their homes the spirit of a female shaman from a neighbouring clan. This female deity remained there to look after the weal and woe of both clans, so when the clan worshipped its own shamanic spirits, they had to simultaneously worship this guest deity, hoping that they would be blessed and protected by both. The two clans probably originated from the same ancient tribe and so give us a glimpse into clan evolution and development.

Some northern peoples, the primitive Manchu in particular, long held traditions of burial in the earth, cremation, and wind burial, as well as bird and beast burial – that is, abandoning the corpse of the deceased to birds and beasts in the wild. Before the concept of souls emerged, the dead were simply abandoned in this way. People would sometimes cover the corpse with a layer of earth, but they mostly left it exposed to be pecked at and borne off by eagles, crows, or wild beasts, the remains eventually being scattered everywhere. Since souls have traditionally been believed to lay hidden in bones, when the bones were scattered abroad in this kind of burial, the souls of the ancestors were believed to reside in all directions to protect and bless the land where their offspring dwelt.

With the development in society, however, people could not bear to cast out the corpses of their loved ones in the wilderness, and with the development of the soul concept, people came to respect the sacred bones of the deceased as having hidden within them the soul. They thus preferred wind burial or cremation. In shamanic belief, wind has its source in *qi* (气, "breath," "air," "gas," or "material energy," "life force," "energy flow," the active principle of any living thing), and *qi* is the essence of a mobilized soul. So wind burial can help souls soar up to the nine heavens or descend to the dwelling places of their descendants. Cremation was also widespread. It came to be thought that the soul hidden in the bones could remain forever only through cremation's cleansing by fire, which could exorcise evil and preserve the good. Teeth are the most difficult to incinerate, so it was believed that a person's immortal soul may also be hidden in one's teeth. After cremation, the teeth were thus hung around a shaman's neck as prayer amulets, kept in a sacred basket, coffer, or pot or hidden in the hollow of a tree behind the family home as the ancestral shrine. Later, there came to be a combination of wind burial and cremation, the former mostly for children, the latter for adults. In any case, the preservation of the cremated remains of the deceased for ancestor worship appeared much later than the use ancestral idols and material objects. It became common among northern peoples in recent centuries.

There have been great differences in the customs of different clans. According to the Manchu heroic folktale *Legends of Nurhaci and Wanggao* (*Liangshi hanwang zhuan*) about the overthrow of the Ming dynasty in the early 17th century, clans living in the basin of the Sungari and its tributary at Harbin the Ashi River often used water burial – casting the corpse into the sea or river to be carried away in the flowing water. People usually wrapped the corpse in fur or thatch, sprinkled wine, and offered animal sacrifice while shamans prayed; or they would tie the corpse to a stone, a stone idol, a pig, a sheep, or something else and throw it into deep water to let it sink to the bottom. Water and sea burial could be performed in either winter or summer.

In shamanist belief, the safest dwelling place is the world of water, a blessed place where deities live and keep the waters in peace and quiet. The *Legend of King Hailing* (*Hailingwang chuanqi*) reports that the consort of Emperor Wanyan Liang, prince of Hailing, fourth emperor of the Jin dynasty, was buried in the Ashi River but became frozen in the river ice in a sudden June snowstorm. Rebellious officials wanted to burn her corpse while the emperor was away in Yandi, but it was firmly protected by the hard ice and could not be burnt. When the emperor came back, he saw his consort in the ice as if she were still alive. Therefore, it was believed that water and ice can keep souls from corruption for centuries and that when souls of the dead cannot find a peaceful dwelling place or come back to earth to check the living conditions of their descendants, they often stop, swim, or hide in water. In any case, when the Manchu and other northern peoples began to settle down, they cultivated the tradition of water and sea sacrifice, and from the Jin dynasty onwards, they would offer animal and even human sacrifice. When shamans worshipped their ancestral gods, they often summoned them in the form of water animals like the otter, seal, turtle, freshwater carp, lizard, or frog. They would dive into the water, claiming that this would make the deities appear or allow them to exorcise evil spirits. Even until now in *ye* rites[2] for worshipping deities of nature, Manchu shamans of many clans display ritual feats such as *zuanbingya* (钻冰崖, the test for a shaman initiate to go through nine ice holes in the river), *tanhaixue* (探海穴, diving into the sea to search a sea cave), and *shuixia mozhen* (水下摸针, diving into the sea to grope for needles). Both the performing shaman and the audience think that these sacred feats can be performed only through the help of the mystic power of the spirits of deceased ancestors or shamans.

The spirit idols used in shamanic ancestor worship are unique and are thought to be powerful. They are made of wide-ranging materials of various shapes: wood, stone, clay, leather, silk, plants, animal bones and fur, fish bones and scales, and so on. With carved eyes, nose, and mouth, they stand for various types of ancestors. *The Goldi* documents that almost every house in that area of Russia had a wooden statuette with two giant breasts or had a pair of statues – man and woman. The 1891 Qing work *Annals of Jilin* (*Jinlin tongzhi*), vol. 27, recounts that in Sanxing (三姓, present-day Yilan, Heilongjiang), there were numerous trees but that they could not be cut down, because they were reserved for carving ancestor effigies. People would carve a human head that had eyes and brows on a piece of wood about one *chi* (尺, 33 centimetres) in length and place it in a corner of the house. Some families had more than ten such wooden idols and regarded them as their ancestors. They would worship them several times a year with a deer sacrifice.

The effigies were thought to have great power, and if a guest mistakenly offended one of them, they would suffer from glaucoma and be blind for several days. No prayer could bring about a recovery. As described in *Old Jilin Records* (*Jinlin jiuwenlu*), the Gilyak people (present-day Nivkh) mentioned in a 12th-century chronicle as inhabiting the Amur estuary worshipped their deceased loved ones with wood effigies that had carved eyes and mouth. They would dress them in bear skin and stick food on the mouth as an offering whenever they ate (Wei Shenghe et al. 1986). The Japanese scholar Torii Ryuzo found that in a small bronze figurine from a Jin dynasty city in northeast China, there is a hole which was probably for threading, to hang the figurine around one's neck as an amulet. Present-day Mongols preserve and worship similar bronze figurines, called *wengget*.

The Oroqen traditionally sacrificed a boar to their ancestral god Ajioru Borukan to pray for an ill clansperson's quick recovery. The Daur had as their ancestor deity the Huozhuor, a female deity worshipped mostly in individual *mukūn* ("subclan"), but also as the common ancestral deity of several *mukūn*, the primogenitor of all the Daur. The Ewenki call their ancestral clan god Sewenki. According to legend, when human beings were first born on earth, there was an Ewenki man with a long braid who found a lake named Lama in a mountain near the Lena River. Around the lake were many mountains, and in it were numerous beautiful flowers, along with hares and snake, and also a giant cave. The case was considered the source of clouds and mist, and it harboured a two-headed snake 75 *chi* long, which came from heaven and was sacred. The cave was said to be the birthplace of the Ewenki people, and the man with the long braid was named Sewenki after his death by his descendants. Regarded as a god, he was also called Malu, and his soul was traditionally enshrined in the form of a human-shaped wooden spirit idol. For their part, the Qibaqi of Inner Mongolia have as their ancestral god Ojiaole, meaning "root." The ancestor was reportedly struck dead by lightning, and he is depicted on a blue cloth, eyebrows made of squirrel fur, along with the sun, the moon, and nine little figures – five golden female ones and four silver male ones. People traditionally implore Ojiaole to exorcise ghosts and treat illness, and they tell him not to be annoyed by his descendants.

The images of ancestors worshipped by northern peoples are depicted mostly in paintings. The Manchu, the Hezhe, and especially the Nanai (Hezhe) north of the Amur are keen on painting their ancestor gods. All kinds of mountains, forests, dragons, birds, snakes, tigers, leopards, frogs, and so on of the world around them are displayed in the paintings. The images of Manchu ancestors came to be elaborately painted with the sun, moon, sacred birds, fine steeds, and herds of animals, and the other world where they dwell is also intricately portrayed, as if they are living the same life they used to live. With the development of modern society, however, all such images have become simplified. To worship their ancestors, the Manchu and other peoples commonly fold multicoloured swaths of silk or satin cloth into squares and kneel before them, and the Manchus and Mongols sometimes also use sacred plaques or embroidered strips of cloth. They hang up yellow satin curtains and place four or five trays of incense in front of the plaques or painted strips of silk cloth in the same way as they do for wooden spirit tablets. The spirit cloths are called *siren* in Manchu, and they vary in colour and number with each clan. Some Manchu families use only these strips, no other representations.

The Manchu, the Xibe, and other peoples traditionally performed *huansuo* as a symbol of the ancestors' protection and blessing of children as a stage in the rite honouring Fodo Mama, the Manchu ancestral goddess of fertility and protector of children. The shaman places a string of colourful threads called *suo* (索, chain) around the neck of a young child. If the child is a girl, the threads will make her grow up healthy and beautiful; if it is a boy, he will become a hero. The Xibe have a rite honouring goddess of fertility Xili Mama that has much in common with the Manchu rite honouring Fodo Mama. The Oroqen have also traditionally worshipped Fodo Mama, and the Daur worship a goddess of fertility, who will be discussed in a subsequent chapter.

Some of the ancestral deities of the Manchu, Oroqen, and other northern peoples are hero gods called *manni* ("hero" in Manchu, probably an ancient Tungus word) or phonetic derivatives of *manni*, such as *malu*, *manye*, and *mangni*.[3] In life, the heroes made great achievements or outstanding contributions to their clans as masters of martial arts, acrobatics, music, dance, archery, or other skills. Some could perform magic, foretell weal and woe, teach music and dance, or tell stories of the clan history. In worshipping Manni or Malu, people would commonly use the sacred idols or utensils used by the heroes in worshipping their ancestors. They venerated them as the wise men of the whole ethnic group, but each clan preserved numerous Malu as their own deities, some clans having dozens of names for them. The fact that *manni* is probably an ancient Tungus word suggests that these hero deities have been worshipped and passed down for ages.

3.2 Worship of fertility deities

Notwithstanding the views of many scholars in the past, goddesses of fertility have always held a prominent position in northern shamanism. In the primordial period, the vast wilderness of northern China was sparsely populated, and fertility and reproduction were vital to every tribe. All people, primitive and modern, domestic and abroad, emphasize fertility and regard praying for babies as a meaningful activity. Archaeological excavations show that this was the case among the early inhabitants of northern China. *Ancient Cultures of Siberia* reveals that the worship of female fertility was prominent. Figures carved out of limestone have frequently been found in areas of the Amur River basin as relics from the Neolithic Age. The most prominent is that of a female ancestral deity. There are nude female figures, three of which have breasts and pudenda that are greatly exaggerated and foregrounded. Stone male phalluses have also been found (Jilin Archaeological Research Office 1975). This reveals that the worship of productive organs occupied a prominent position in both matriarchal societies and patriarchal societies and that fertility worship played an important role in primitive belief in the region.

In 1982, Chinese archaeologists found similar artefacts in areas southeast of the Dachengzi, Mongolian autonomous county, Liaoning Province and on both banks of the Daling River of that region. Altogether, over twenty fragments of red pottery figures were unearthed, most of them with human shapes. They fall into two categories: two small upright, pregnant nude figures whose heads and right arms are missing, and figures with curved bellies, bulky hips, bent left arms, right hands on the upper belly, and marks showing their pudenda. These are bulky figures of polished loess with round bellies and slightly bent lower limbs, all with a red glaze.

In excavations between 1983 and 1985, Chinese archaeologists working in Niuheliang Village, western Liaoning, found a temple dedicated to a goddess, several groups of large stone graves, and the remains of square, castle-like stone walls covering an area of 40,000 square metres. These remains are believed to be five thousand years old, and from them precious antique symbols of matriarchal clan society have been unearthed: small nude female pottery figurines and the life-size coloured heads of goddesses, as well as a batch of clay fragments of nude female figures of various sizes. At the Dongshanzui altar site at Niuheliang Village, two small ceramic figurines of pregnant nude women with curved bellies, bulky hips, bent left arms, left hands on the abdomen, and triangular markings on the pudenda were unearthed. Some experts think they are goddesses of fertility; others that they were used as sacrificial offerings.[4]

In 1984, I came upon an eagle-headed nude female spirit idol in Yangpao Village, Huichun, the Yanbian Korean autonomous prefecture, Jilin Province, whose height is 50 centimetres and breasts are prolapsed like straps. She is breastfeeding an infant in her arms and has a curved belly and clearly exposed pudenda. A hereditary spirit idol preserved by the Manchu He clan, it is kept hidden in a secret sacred coffer and allowed to be taken out only when the clan shaman (originally female but later male) prayed for babies, breast milk, or an easy delivery or performed an exorcism before labour. The shaman would then worship the idol, burn incense, and conduct prayers. The similar eagle-headed, woman-bodied eagle princess goddess mentioned earlier has been regarded as the first goddess of fertility and as the primogenitor of shamans.

According to Zhao Xingya, an elder of the Manchu Zhao clan from a small village in Yongji County, Jilin, the primogenitor deity left three deities to humankind: Fohemu (pudendum), Dodokv (penis) and Tvhhongwu (fire bell). Passed down from generation to generation, their spirit idols are hung as clay pendants on shamans' breasts and have been worshipped for ages. Another fertility deity is the Manni spirit idol kept in a sacred coffer over the west *kang* kept by the Manchu Guan, Luo, and other clans in a sacred coffer over the west *kang* (炕, heatable raised brick bed platform in homes of northeastern China). The figure is broad at the top and narrow at the bottom, shaped ▲, without eyes, mouth, or nose. It is the goddess of fertility in charge of curing sterility in both males and females and ensuring birth to newlyweds who worship it.

Snakes have commonly been viewed as protective fertility deities. Fertility needs warmth and sunshine to breed and flourish, and snakes are regarded

as related to the sun god. The Chuokuo Manni worshipped by some clans is a column-shaped spirit idol enclosed by a lifelike raising snake head.

These figures are recorded in *Sacred Book of the Manchu Fire Ritual of the Seven Hulun Clans* (*Hulun qixing manzhou huoji shengshu*) from the sixteenth year of the reign of the Guangxu emperor (1891) of the Qin dynasty as the "divine words of fire sacrifice" of the Seven Hulun Clan Alliance of Jurchen tribes in the late 16th century.[5]

Fodo Mama, goddess of fertility and protector of children, occupies an important position in Manchu rites. Some clans have worshipped her in the form of a spirit idol shaped like a nude woman. In the Na clan of Yangpao Village, along with a hereditary wooden figurine of this goddess, there is also worshipped a goddess called Wanli Mama, who has care of female fertility, needlework, and cooking. Legend has it that she is naked and leads a horse. Only shamans are allowed to see her effigy and only when a sacrificial ritual is held (Peng Bo 1996:130–131).

As is noted in early Manchu mythology, the dominant male god of heaven and the universe Abka Enduri was initially the female deity Abka Hehe. *Hehe* means "woman" in Manchu, and its etymological Manchu root is *fefe*, "pudendum," pointing to female fertility. At that time, the image of Abka Hehe was a pudendum shaped like a willow leaf, signifying that the goddess gives birth to everything. Primordial human beings saw a resemblance between willow leaves and pudenda, so mythology has it that willows gave birth to human beings and the world. According to a shaman's inspired utterances of the Manchu Sitara Hala of Huichun, ancient Manchu people thus venerated willows as standing for the primogenitor deity. When Abka Hehe fought with the demon Yeluli, many good deities died, and Abka Hehe had no choice but to ascend up to heaven. Yeluli was close behind and grabbed hold of her battle dress, which was made of willow leaves. A handful of the leaves were stripped off, floated down to earth, and gave birth to humankind and the world.

Another myth regarding willows is contained in an oracle of the Fuca Hala of Mudanjiang, Heilongjiang, whose early ancestors lived by the Hurhan River:

> In ancient times, the Hurhan River suddenly turned into the Hurhan Sea, and all creatures were drowned in the flood. Of all the persons made of mud by Abka Enduri, only one was left. About to drown as he floated on the rushing

> water, he survived by grabbing a willow branch that bore him into a stone cave which stood halfway in the water. The branch then turned into a beautiful woman who had intercourse with him and bore offspring.

In this story, the willow takes on strong overtones of the clan totem, and in the past, Fuca clanspeople set a willow branch in a sacred container and worshipped it. They picked a new willow each year when the *jia* ritual was held and sent the old branch floating down the river with great reverence. This yearly ritual has passed down their ancestors' belief in the female primogenitor deity to modern times.

The prominent function of every clan shaman is to use their mystic power to treat illness and dispel misfortune, and for this, they have always been highly respected by their clanspeople. Even until modern times, many shamans have still had unique curative powers, which they kept to themselves. It cannot be assumed that such powers are a matter of mere fantasy. If that were the case, the shamans would have long been mistrusted by their clanspeople and abandoned. According to our interviews with dozens of experienced and newly initiated shamans among various northern peoples, the two most prominent functions of a shaman are to ward off evil spirits and pray for fertility. Shamans are said to have traditionally given advice on coitus techniques, including those based mainly on physiology: what kind of man and woman can have successful intercourse, when they should do so, and so on. According to scattered Manchu folktales and epic narratives such as the *Record of the Grievances of the East Sea*, the *Secret Records of the Shunzhi and Kangxi* (*Shun kang milu*), and *Umesiben Mama* and according to accounts of senior shamans of many clans, in the days of primitive society, people knew nothing about how to have intercourse, conceive, and go into labour, all of which were considered strange and mystical. Some had intercourse with people of the same sex because they believed that "only if two persons are physically united does the god bring babies." This was a rudimentary instinct expressed in oracles.

In those ancient times, group marriage and incestual unions were not uncommon, but as society developed, marriage became exogamous and later monogamous. According to clan principles, a female shaman, not the clan chieftain, executed divine authority to control and manage exogamous unions and guard against incest within the clan. She officiated at the marriages of her clanspeople, by saying ritual prayers. People who violated clan marriage rules were punished, which guaranteed the prosperity of clan offspring and averted malformation and degeneration. Men and women could not live together in exogamous unions without the permission of the shamans of both clans. In matriarchal society, a woman married a man from another clan, and he was dependent on her. The union commonly took the form of a reciprocal exchange sanctioned by a shaman's inspired utterances, and it was often with a man captured from another tribe. In patriarchal society, marriages arranged by shamans were more common and solemn. When a man married a woman from a different clan, the couple first had to worship heaven and the ancestors at the ancestral shrine.

Shamans have commonly performed ablutions for a new couple, often at night. Holding a sacred wand and ritual *hama* (knife) in their hands, the shaman would poke and press at the couple's naked parts while chanting. This was a form of acupunctural *dianxue* known as *dim mak* (pressing the pulse). Sometimes, tuberose, mug wort, or perilla leaves were spread under the couple; rhododendron was burnt, and the couple would take powder processed from the penis of a fur seal.

Shamans have possessed special massage skills for curing infertility, and to cure impotence and infertility, some used powder made from talcum, agaric, earthworms, or beehives and others from the baked and dried male genitals of a Mongolian gazelle, dog, badger, or bear. While praying, they would have the couple take the powder as a cure. Steaming and washing one's waist and perineum with bear or tiger urine was also used to treat impotence and infertility. Female shamans often treated the couple at night through a *beideng* ritual (背灯祭, Manchu night rite with all the lights out) while a *zaili* assistant beat a drum fiercely and burnt mug wort. The afflicted couple would close their eyes and get undressed. Then the shaman would apply *dianxue* pressure and massage in a rite known as the descent of the Kvgvmu deity, and in this atmosphere, the couple would then take medicine with water.

Shamans have also had special skills in dealing with problems during childbirth. The Daur *balecin* shaman was actually a midwife who helped correct the position of the fetus and deliver a baby (Qiu Pu 1985:88). The Manchu megashaman Wu Xulun (吴绪伦) of Ulajie, Jilin Province, could cure gynaecological diseases. In the past, female shamans of the Li clan from Bohai Xiang (village) of Ning'an could deal with a woman's difficult labour. Shamans of the Zhang clan in Sunwu, Heilongjiang, could likewise treat infertility and deal with difficult birth. Shamans were traditionally the closest thing to doctors for healthcare for a woman or child and the only physician of the whole clan. They performed medical treatment according to the mystical descent and prophetic oracles of the gods, and they performed some important operations and acupuncture treatments in a boisterous ritual environment that could distract patients' attention and alleviate their pain in a state of semiconsciousness. When patients recovered, they believed they were cured by the god, not by the shaman.

When shamans performed a healing rite to deal with infertility caused by intestinal gas or poor blood circulation, they would place dozens of leeches on a sacred drum, their waist bells, and the patient's belly and legs. They would then drum continuously and chant loud spirit chants. When leeches suck out the poison in the patient, they swell up and die, and the patient is restored to health. Northern shamanic rites praying for fertility include the *zisi* rite to pray for children's well-being, the *yuyun* ritual to pray for childbirth, the Jianying ritual to pray for a baby's health, the *duozi* ritual to pray for many offspring (especially male offspring), and so on. When exploring the various forms of shamanic fertility worship, we should attach great importance to goddesses of childbirth and the protection of children. Early in the 20th century, two statues of such goddesses – Cuisheng Niangniang and Songsheng Niangniang – were found in the Niangniang Temple built during the reign of Qing Emperor Qianglong (乾隆, 1736–1796). One is raising an infant with both hands while another baby is beside her legs; the other carries a bag on her back, from which many infant heads are emerging. The Han Chinese also had their own goddesses of fertility (Ivanov 1990).

Among the Ewenki and other northern peoples, fertility deities are often worshipped as Umai (Umay, from the old Jurchen word *umusi*). Umai is a goddess who protects babies and whose effigy is a sparrow made of birch or larch, but the term can also refer to a child's soul, which, as we have said, is thought to be a little sparrow. When a child is seriously ill, it is thought that the soul has left the child's body and gone to another world, so that it must be retrieved by a shaman in a trance dance (Inner Mongolia Editorial Committee 1986a:233).

I researched into the etymology of the names of some deities. Those of some deities in charge of childbirth and the protection of infants are similar among various Siberian peoples. When women desire to have a baby, they traditionally ask the following goddesses for help:

Tungus Manchu
Aomai – woman's belly, uterus (Ewenki)
Aomo – nest, cave, hole (Nanai)
Wumuke – nest (Ewenki in the Turpan area of Xinjiang)
Aomi – soul of one-year-old infant (Negidal)
Aomiya – soul of a one-year-old infant (Nanai)
Aomisong Mama – clan tree where the souls of children grow in this goddess's heavenly abode (Nanai)
Aomi (Umi) and Aomixi (Umisi) goddesses having the care of infants (Ewenki in northeast China)

Turkic and Mongol
Aomai – woman's belly, uterus (Khalkha, Inner Mongolia)
Umai – woman's belly, uterus (Mongol)
Umai – placenta (Buryat in Zabaykalsky Krai, Russia)
Umai – amulet protecting babies from misfortune and evil spirits (Kachin)
Emai – protective deity of children (Beltir)
Umai, Emai, Mai – protective goddesses of infants (Shor, Teleut and Khakas)

According to these names, the basic term "Umai" has been used with diversified phonetic pronunciations and meanings, but it refers mostly to the goddess of fertility who protects babies. Quite reasonable is the early Tungus-Manchu etymological explanation of the term as meaning "nest" or "cave," referring to the nest of infants, a woman's uterus or belly. The worship of female fertility grew into the worship of childbearing, which in turn evolved into the worship of a goddess who cares for children's souls.

Ancient Siberian peoples thus understood "Umai" in terms of female fertility, and this belief evolved among the Ewenki, such that the term "Umai" came to refer to the soul of a *tongzi* (young child). However, we hold the view that "Umai" originally referred to the worship and celebration of mystic female fertility as being more powerful than that of a man and deserving of great reverence in line with ideas of matriarchal society. Among the Manchu along the Amur, there are still words with a pronunciation similar to "Umai," in particular the term for the goddess of fertility

Umi. Legend has it that Umi was transmitted from mother to daughter as a goddess related to menstruation. The original image and the original concept of Umai have been preserved in folklore, but the meaning and the power have changed.

Notes

1 Standardized form of the Manchu shamanic ritual in the mid Qing dynasty as influenced by Qing court rituals. It does not involve spirit possession, and it is not necessarily a family rite, though *jia* 家 basically means "home" or "family."

2 *Ye* rites (*yeji*, 野祭) are Manchu shaman rites, including possession, inviting a god, and sending off the god.

3 Among the Mongols and Daur, Manni is called *manggai* or *mangus*; among the Oroqen and Ewenki, *mangai* or *mangni*; among other Manchu clans, *mahus* or *mahu*; and among the Hezhe, *mahu*.

4 See *Guangming Daily* 光明日报, July 25, 1986.

5 The seven clans are Husihali Hala, Namdulu Hala, Nimaca Hala, Hexeri Hala, Cigujila Hala, Sumri Hala, and Niohuru Hala.

4 Blood sacrifice and fire rituals

Shamanism features sacrificial worship of various types and styles as a manifestation of its beliefs and ideas about nature and human existence. The motley collection of its sacrificial rituals can be viewed as a kaleidoscope of history, religion, and culture. We have long had little understanding of the various rites, styles, rules, and taboos of shamanic culture, and we have wrongly assumed that many of the northern clans' sacrificial forms and methods are very much the same – simplistic and monotonous – and that there is no need for further serious study. In fact, this has hampered our objective understanding and study of shamanism. As a primitive form of religion, shamanism expresses its unpretentious forms of primitive theism mainly in ceremonies and rituals. Unfortunately, with the passage of time, the details in the rites have been largely forgotten. This chapter summarizes and sorts out typical Chinese shaman rites and their ritual modes in order to discuss the significance, status, and value that shamanism deserves in the history of human culture. *Discourses of the States* (*Guoyu*), the collection of speeches from the spring and autumn period (771–476 BCE), documents that in times of yore human beings and spirits did not intermingle but that certain human individuals were more perspicacious, single-minded, and venerable than others. Their powers of comprehension enabled them to make meaningful comparisons between what lay above and below, and their insights into things enabled them to perceive what was remote and profound. It was upon these gifted people that the gods and spirits would descend. If male, they were called *xi* (覡, shamans) and, if female, *wu* (巫, shamanesses). At that time, the boundaries between the divine and the mundane were distinct. The gods accepted people's ritual offerings and blessed them in return, so that there were no natural calamities and no want of wealth and goods. Later, however, it is said that the nine prehistoric Jiuli tribes of the Yangtze River basin led by the mythical Chiyou[1] abandoned the rites, which led to disorder in the world and the intermingling of humans and gods.

The *Book of Rites* (*Liji*)[2] records that in ancient historical times, people worshipped heaven by burning oblations on a pile of wood at the Taitan altar, in a southern suburb of the capitol; and they worshipped the earth by burying oblations near the Taishe altar in a northern suburb. As an offering to the seasons, they buried a sheep and a pig near the Taizhao altar, and to exorcise evil, they offered sacrifices to the gods of cold and heat in a *kan* (pit) or on a *tan* (mound).

They sought blessings from the sun at the Wanggong altar, implored favour from the moon at the Yeming altar, payed reverence to the stars at Youyong, and made peace with the spirits of flood and drought at Yuyong. People established a *kan* and *tan* in each of the four directions – north, south, east, and west – to express their reverence for the gods of the four cardinal directions. They believed gods or spirits oversee mountains, forests, streams, valleys, hills, and mounds, which can produce clouds, winds, and rain but can also make monsters appear. State sovereigns would offer sacrifices to them all.

In ancient China, people celebrated the *laba* ritual (*labaji*, 腊八祭) on the eighth day of the La month (Layue腊月), the twelfth month of the Chinese lunar calendar, in which they offered sacrifices to the earth, plants, insects, animals, and all the other objects on earth, in accordance with the primitive religious practices of the Huaxia (华夏, ancestral Han tribes). With the growing number of deities, the ritual procedures of the rite became more and more elaborate (Ding Shan 1988:4). So "taxes from the *Bangdu* area were used for sacrificial rituals" (Cui Gaowei 1997), and various ritual chants and sacrificial texts appeared.

The ritual types and styles of primordial shamanism were, no doubt, broadly similar to what I just wrote. In the past, it was not possible to substantiate the various types and styles, but progress in the field has been made on the basis of legends and the recollections of senior shamans. We have discovered traces of the types and styles in old texts that are the cultural heritage of the Manchu, Xibe, Oroqen, and Daur peoples.[3] Many of the sacred teachings in these documents are incorporated in the *jao'uyun* training programme for Manchu shaman initiates. They are related to specific ritual procedures and have been carefully written down and bound into records because of ancestors' worries that their posterity would neglect them.

4.1 Blood sacrifice

According to such records, the most ancient shamanic ritual was solemn blood sacrifice, and that tradition has been preserved among the Ewenki, Oroqen, Manchu, and Xibe ethnic groups. According to the *Records of Sacrificial Rules and Procedures of the Fu Clan* (*Fushi jigui chengshi lixulu*), people of the clan should not forget the ancestral sacrificial rules. Shamans should perform a trance dance, choose an auspicious day, and offer sacrifice to the goddesses of the night in the *beideng* ritual, to the gods of the day in the *yuan* ritual, and gods of mountains and rivers in the *shanhe* ritual. They offer the hearts of certain animals and an adequate amount of blood of the finest animals. Among the various rituals, the *shanhe* ritual became solidified early. It involved primarily the worship of these deities of the wilds in line with the early consciousness of primitive human beings in their hostile living conditions. At the earliest stage of development, the sacrificial offerings were not limited to particular domesticated or wild animals, but the preferred choice was wild boar and elk, and people who lived by fishing or hunting along waterways sacrificed fish or birds. The *Uyun Divine Words of the Qian Clan* (*Qianxing wuyun shenyu*) recounts that clan ancestors had for many a generation lived along the old estuary of the Huichun River, a tributary of the Tumen River near the easternmost point of Jilin Province. Legend has it that the ancestors made their houses on tree tops, where they lived all year long. When they offered sacrifice, they preferred deer, ducks, geese, and fish. On the occasion of the *beideng* ritual to the goddesses of night, all the clanspeople would line the river on a starry night and keep nine bonfires blazing so that the river was lit up as bright as day. The female shaman officiant wore a ritual costume made of white fish scales and white clam shells, with numerous white beads on her forehead and white scapula bones tied around her waist as bells. People packed deer, ducks, geese, huge Siberian salmon, and sometimes several captive boars on a boat, and more than a dozen people sprinkled animal blood on them to send a sign of their faithfulness to the woods, wilderness, rivers, heaven, earth, and rocks. They would smear their bodies, waists, and foreheads with blood and then make a fire to roast the sacrificial meat, which was shared by all. At dawn, they threw the remaining offerings into the river to drift away. The Qian *beideng* rite has a long history, and it was determined that it not fall into oblivion. Clan records are quite detailed. The sacrificial blood was sprinkled not only on mountains and rivers but also on all participants, from which we can see that offering blood was regarded as the grandest moment of the rite.

Blood offerings were traditionally indispensable in northern shaman rites, with blood symbolizing clanspeoples' deep reverence for their deities. Shamans from the Zang and Wu clans, along with the Oroqen shaman Mo Fusheng (莫福生) and Daur shaman Wu Dekun (吴德坤) stated that the blood of wild animals was sacrificed in their *beideng* rituals. Pots, baskets, and all other containers were smeared with blood, and the foreheads and bodies of clanspeople and women suffering from chronic disease or making a prolonged recovery were smeared with the blood to exorcise the cause of their illness and dispel evil. In addition, people would add a few drops of blood to water or wine and then gulp it down as a propitious drink. They would also smear blood on the mouths of spirit idols and figurines of the Manni hero deity mentioned in the previous chapter and sometimes even on furniture and livestock. To this day, a thick layer of black and red marks can still be detected on long-cherished spirit idols made of deer hide, cloth, or wood, which master shamans say are traces of the smeared blood. In the early years of the Republic of China (1912–1949), a master shaman of the Zang clan once refused to drink ordinary water or rice wine when a god possessed him but drank only animal blood from a big clay bowl, and when a master shaman of the He clan of Huichun was possessed, he would drink the blood of wild ducks and swans.

Rites of drinking and smearing blood are documented in almost every Manchu clan. Blood sacrifice has not been common in modern times, but the *beideng* ritual could still be observed among various northern peoples, with the blood of slaughtered animals offered to nature deities, totem deities, or ancestor deities – all punctuated by smearing blood on the mouths of spirit idols and statuettes. Ritual instruments and sacred poles were also painted with a little blood. After the rite, the blood was always consumed, never discarded. Some people dribbled blood into water, which they sprinkled in houses and barns and around gates to exorcise evil. They dripped the remaining blood into wine, which they then drank or made into pancakes or blood sausages.

For their part, the Mongols traditionally celebrated a grand blood sacrifice on Dokdor Mountain on the Songnen Plain bordering Inner Mongolia and Heilongjiang after dusk on a set day during the summer flood period:

> The shaman presided over the ceremony by igniting nine bonfires and chanting sacred chants accompanied by his drumming and dancing. He would commonly stand in front of the crowd and perform miraculous feats of magic. The tribal chieftain would deliver prayers to the mountain god to express gratitude for the god's blessing. He would then splash three bowls of milk liquor in the direction of the mountain peak and slay a black horse as a blood sacrifice. They would bind the horse's four legs with its head pointed toward the mountain and then chop its face with an axe. Spurting toward the peak, the blood was offered to the mountain. For hundreds of years, through several dynasties, this sacrificial ritual of worshipping Dokdor Mountain has never ceased.
>
> (Bo Shaobu 1987:33)

In rites of the northern Daur, a shaman would mix ox blood with milk or wine, which was then ladled into wooden bowls. At the same time, two shamans would invite the gods to descend to earth to enjoy the blood while the clanspeople beat drums and followed the shamans in dance. The shamans mimicked the chirping of birds, indicating that the deities turned into birds to drink the blood. Meanwhile, people smeared ox blood on the mouths of the spirit idols and deity statuettes one by one, indicating that the gods had drunk the blood (Cai Jiaqi 1988). The Oroqen held a sacrificial blood rite to worship the mountain god Bainata. The Ewenki celebrated solemn blood rites that had numerous taboos. Hunters should not cut into arteries when they were skinning a bear, so as not to cause loss of blood. Instead, they squeezed arterial blood into the bear's heart. They then tied up its head, throat, tongue, nose, neck bone, foot bones, and ribs with birch and smeared them all with blood and pigments from wildflowers as a grand wind burial for the bear. They also used the blood of deer or elk. When shamans performed a trance dance to treat illness, they would choose white reindeer or elk as an offering, erect a stake in front of the *sierranju* dwelling,[4] and smear the stake with reindeer blood (Inner Mongolia Editorial Committee 1986a). In the Xibe initiation *chakur* ritual of climbing a ladder of sharp knives, before climbing it, shaman initiates had to take a swig of sheep blood, which signified that they were blessed by the gods, made brave and invincible (He Ling 1990:106).

These sacred blood sacrifices have a long history, dating from the primeval period when it was believed that blood is life. During their struggles with fierce animals and creatures in the wilds, people realized that if they bled, humans and animals alike, they would soon die. In time, this fact led them to appreciate the sanctity of the red liquid coursing through their veins and the veins of other living creatures. In ancient burial rites, live pigs, dogs, deer, and other animals were put in the exterior coffin of the deceased, probably for the sake of their blood. Older coffins were painted with blood and later ones with red paint or similar material, symbolizing that they were covered with blood – hence the red powder found the archaeological excavations of the Upper Cave of Dragon Bone Hill in Beijing in the 1930s. The shamanic idea is that blood or red is an omen of life and vitality.

The belief that in dreams floating souls can travel outside the body might have inspired a similar understanding of blood: if it drains out of the body, the soul will get lost and go astray. For northern peoples, it is thus quite inauspicious if a common utensil is smeared with blood: it is feared that one day the blood will transform into evil spirits. This ancient notion and its corresponding taboo reflect northern peoples' belief that blood has life and can become an independent vital agent. Consequently, up until modern times, apart from blood sacrifice, northern peoples have normally avoided staining furniture with human or animal blood, believing that it may cause misfortune.

Ancient Chinese texts speak of the life-giving power of blood. The legendary *Chunqiu Hechengtu*, a 17th-century history of ancient China, tells of a girl born on Blood Rock. She was Qingdu, daughter of the divine Jade emperor (Yu emperor 玉帝) and mother of the mythic Emperor Yao. One day, when there was much thunder and lightning, blood penetrated into the huge rock, and from this Qingdu was born. Another ancient text, the medical treatise *Yellow Emperor's Canon of Medicine* (*Huangdi neijing*), supposedly from 2600 BCE, states that blood and *qi* are the essence of life. The 251 CE text *Book of Later Han: Biography of Deng Zhi* (*Houhanshu denzhi zhuan*) speaks of slaughtering animals and sacrificing their blood to the gods. According to the ancient *Rites of Zhou* (*Zhouli*),[5] people held blood sacrifice to the gods of soil and grain, to the variously identified "five deities" of ancient China, and to the five great mountains.[6] In the oral traditions of northern peoples, moreover, there are numerous legends and folktales in which clean blood is transformed into good spirits, whereas contaminated blood becomes evil spirits.

Because it was thought that blood can make the earth fertile and fruitful, blood sacrifice became an established custom among northern peoples when they first settled down and began to farm. Accordingly, in the famous Manchu folktale "Daffodil Princess" (*Shuixian gege*), when the princess is killed by a serpent demon, her red blood spurts over farmlands that then yield myriad ears of the maize that is so common in northern China (Fu Yuguang 1984). In traditional *jia* rituals, the Manchu and other peoples worshipped the seedling god, who had charge of farming. They would butcher animals and sprinkle their blood on the ground and towards heaven as a prototype of later earth worship.

According to the *Record of the Grievances of the East Sea*, humans, not animals, were killed, buried, or drowned in some celebrations of the sea burial rite. In other cases, prisoners of war from enemy clans were killed and their blood offered in sacrifice. In the Manchu epic *Umesiben Mama* the great shamaness Umesiben sacrificed nine heads, nine hands, nine feet, and nine breast bones of the enemy Huduor tribe to the Black Wind Valley in order to seek a blessing that her clanspeople would get free of smallpox. In the eyes of the primitive peoples, prisoners were like captive animals and could be killed as sacrificial offerings. Such human sacrifice could convey a higher degree of respect and piety and so please deities more. Consequently, there are quite a few shamanic legends that centre on human blood or bone sacrifice. In such tales, humans are sacrificed for their blood or bone spirits, and plotlines are added explaining that they were eaten by demons representing hated enemy tribes in an attempt to justify such human sacrifice. The widespread worship of human-eating demons indicates that various northern peoples had experienced a period of barbaric cannibalism in which humans were indeed sacrificed and eaten. The Oroqen, Daur, and Ewenki call such demons *manggai*, *mangai*, or *mangge* (from a Tungus etymological root) and imagine them as having a human form but malformed or with multiple heads, and Manchu folklore speaks of a human-devouring, blood-drinking demon called *mahu* or *mahuzi*. The following is a representation of the spirit idol of a Daur *manggai* carved in wood:

The nine human heads suggest a human-eating demon with invincible might and boldness.

Tragic episodes of blood feuds, the law of the jungle, and survival of the fittest among ancient tribes have been preserved in tales and rituals which inspire fear to this day. As human society progressed, however, human sacrifice and human blood sacrifice soon became abstract descriptions in history books. The custom of offering animal blood to the gods came to be practised in its place and passed down for thousands of years. The parts of animals traditionally used in northern shaman rites are as follows:

1 Domestic animals: bones, flesh, blood, hooves of cattle, horses and sheep.
2 Wild animals: bones, flesh, skin, teeth, blood of tigers, leopards, bears, boars, whales, pythons, and lynxes.
3 Deer: bones, horns, flesh, skin, hooves, blood of deer, elk, roe deer, river deer, red deer, musk deer, Mongolian gazelles, and wild goats.
4 Birds: bones, flesh, quills, feathers, claws, blood of eagles, vultures, ducks, domestic and wild geese, cranes, gulls, pheasants, quail, tomtits, hazel grouses, and great bustards.
5 Small animals: bones, skin, blood of hedgehogs, raccoons, martens, squirrels, and pangolin.
6 Fish: bones, scales, meat, fins, and the blood of various fish in rivers, lakes, and the sea.
7 Aquatic animals: bones, skin, digits, and the blood of otters.

This is only a rough, typical list. In practice, the animals sacrificed varied according to region and ritual purpose. The Indigenous peoples of the Arctic, for example, have traditionally used polar bears, whales, seals, and sealions. They would collect the animals' blood and ritually pour it into the icy sea.

It is clear that shamanism, as a religion stemming from primitive times, believes in blood sacrifice, but what exactly is the relationship between shamanic belief and blood? On the one hand, there is the notion that blood serves as a medium for floating souls to leave the body and roam about. On the other, there is the key concept that the soul dwells in one's blood. It is believed that souls inhabit both bones and blood, that blood makes a soul vigorous, and that the energy life flow of *qi* regulates blood flow. If *qi* is lacking, blood will also be insufficient or dry up. The soul will become feeble and eventually be lost. All in all, primordial shamanism has believed that *qi*, blood, and the soul are closely related and complementary, each relying perpetually on the other for survival.

Moreover, according to shamanism, a human spirit or animal spirit is protected by *qi* and nurtured by blood. This is much like concepts of traditional Chinese medicine: according to *yinqi*, *qi* flows in the blood vessels, complements blood, and has a strong *yin* aspect (feminine, dark, passive, soft, providing spirit), and according to *weiqi*, *qi* is distributed in the skin, muscles, and tissues; serves as a defence mechanism; and has a pronounced *yang* nature (masculine, light, active, hard, providing form to things). Also according to shamanism, *qi* cleanses the path for the spirit and the power of *qi* is enhanced and nurtured by blood. If blood is sufficient; *qi* is vigorous; and if *qi* is vigorous, it can defend and nurture the spirit.

On the basis of simple experience, primitive humans believed that for both humans and animals, blood and life thus enjoy a cause-and-effect relationship upon which all their activities depend. Consequently, they enjoyed drinking fresh animal blood, a practice that may have been learned from blood-eating rodents such as weasels. Many northern peoples drank newly slaughtered deer blood when they were hunting, believing that it could make them fit and strong. The custom of drinking blood was quite common, and people even mistakenly believed that when they lost blood from wounds or injuries, they could retrieve its power by sucking it back into the body.

The concept of blood eating gradually influenced peoples' notions of worship: they believed that if they offered fresh blood to spirits and deities, the spirits and deities would always be around to protect people and their livestock. For that reason, blood has long been considered the most sacred and devote form of worship. Early shamans commonly killed numerous animals the night before offering sacrifice, and the whole ritual became a matter of flesh, bone, and blood sacrifice. Sometimes shamans would drink animal blood as they pricked their own cheeks, hands, feet, and breasts, all while chanting and dancing. When people did not consume all the meat of a blood sacrifice, they would bury the leftovers in the wilderness, mountains, and riverbanks to provide the deities with everlasting food. Followers of Lamaism later condemned this practice as extravagant and wasteful, but believers in shamanism thought differently. When Manchu and other northern clanspeople were sick or faced troubles, they would traditionally summon a shaman to perform blood sacrifice to seek a cure or peace. Even in recent history, a considerable number of clans have held blood rituals for ill patients or the heads of households who were facing difficulties, offering in sacrifice blood drawn by pricking their flesh.

4.2 Fire rituals

Ancient shaman fire rituals aim to praise and worship fire for its beneficence and formidable power to cast off chill, ward off calamites, and exorcise evil. Such rites had far-reaching influences and were quite prevailing. In Chapter 2, we stated the basic concepts of northern fire worship; the present discussion focuses on the materials and procedures traditionally used in the solemn but lively Mongol and Manchu fire rites. The discussion is based mainly on hereditary shamanic texts of various Manchu clans and interviews with elder shamans.

Mongol sacrificial fire rituals were performed in a distinctive atmosphere peculiar to the grazing and hunting culture. The open-air rite mentioned earlier to worship the sacred Dokdor Mountain on the Songnen Plain highlights fire sacrifice as a communal event or household activity. For the communal celebration, all clan members gather at the foot of the mountain after dark and set up their yurts in an august assembly. The presiding shaman first lights nine bonfires, then beats his hand drum, intones sacred chants, and pours three bowls of milk liquor towards the mountain. A black horse is slaughtered in sacrifice, and all kneel before the mountain. Afterwards, people divide into nine groups, which walk around the nine fires clockwise in turn, forming nine circles. As they walk, they pray silently, throw various kinds of dairy foods into the fires, and sprinkle the milk liquor. They normally remain at the site until the bonfires have completely died out. In conjunction with this public rite, each household usually holds a night family ritual to worship the mountain in the hope of obtaining blessings for family members or animals plagued with illness, troubles, or misfortune. People place a small square table in the northwest of the courtyard or yurt, build a fire before it, and offer mutton or a sheep's head in sacrifice. Some offer cream, cheese, dried milk, or milk curds. After setting out their offering, the head of the household or whole family kneel towards the northwest and then throw their offerings into the fire (Bo Shaobu 1987).

According to *Mongol Fire Rituals* (*Mengguzu baihuo xisu gaiguan*) compiled by Wu Yisang (吴依桑) and Bagen, the Mongols have an ancient custom of preserving a live "day fire" for one day, a "month fire" for thirty days, and a "year fire" for a whole year: the longer the more precious. At important family events, such as weddings, funerals, and the beginning of the pasturing and hunting seasons, people first offer liquor and butter at the hearth to pray for the fire god's blessing. On the twenty-third day of the twelfth lunar month, moreover, every household cleans their house and yard and holds the yearly Mongolian family fire ritual. In ancient times, a shaman officiated, but since it was not always practical for shamans to visit each household, the family head could preside. Sometimes, too, lamas of the Yellow Hat sect,[7] which also had fire rituals, but was at odds with shamanism, competed with shamans for the role of presider. Lamas were exclusively in charge of fire worship in the Horqin clan. In any case, the officiant was usually male, and for the sacrifice, males are on the right (the superior position) and females on the left (the inferior position), with the elders in front and younger family members at the rear. The whole family kneel around the hearth, and the host chants the fire eulogy. According to *Appreciation of Mongolian Customs* (*Menggu fengsu jian*), the offerings for a fire sacrifice are mainly whole sheep, *amasi* (meat congee similar to pilaf), red dates, butter, liquor, and a white silk *khata*.[8] After kneeling, the host pours the offerings into the fire in a set order. The state of the flames indicates whether the family will prosper and have a good harvest: the more vigorously the flames dance, the more prosperous the prospects of a good harvest. The Mongolian fire eulogy is quite artful, with the following distinctive ethnic features:

> *Khan!*
> *Mother!*
> *My dear fire-mother!*
> *Here we offer you butter,*
> *Offer you the yellow head of a white sheep,*
> *Offer you fat and oil,*
> *Offer you fermented mare milk kefir!*

The fire ritual is completed after people have worshipped, knelt towards the fire, chanted the eulogy, and offered sacrifice. Afterwards, the whole family sit around the hearth and eat *amasi*, using only black chopsticks, in the "fire meal." Any guest present receives a share of the *amasi* and a chunk of the lamb breast as a sign of sharing in the blessings of the fire god.

For the Manchu shamanic fire rite, manuscripts of its rules and procedures preserved by various clans provide valuable information. The *Sacred Book of the Manchu Fire Ritual of the Seven Hulun Clans* (*Hulun qixing manzhou huoji shengshu*), compiled in 1891 and acquired by scholars in Huichun in the 1980s, is the most important manuscript for understanding the Manchu fire sacrifice during the Qing dynasty. The drive for compiling the document probably came from the gradual simplification of shamanism in the late Qing dynasty. Master shamans from various clans and *mukūn* (paternal subclans that still remain among Manchu-Tungus peoples) then wrote down the contents of the rite for future generations. An analysis of the manuscript as preserved in Huichun indicates that the final segments were recalled from memory after the original had been lost. Nonetheless, it gives us insights into the rite as practised in Qing times. It lists the following standard procedures: summoning of deities and prayer for peace and good health; worship of heaven; chant to raise the fire; *ye* rite; chant of the sacred tree; chant for the fire competition; sacrificial chant; and so on. A Manchu language version is attached as a reference for shamans and their assistant *zaili* when studying the sacrificial texts.

Among the Seven Hulun Clans, the fire rite is called fire rite of the sacred tree. From the manuscript, we learn that it was held mostly on occasions when clan illness, plague, or battles broke out or for injuries from hunting or fishing. The *mukūnda* (subclan chief) and all the clan master shamans would then perform the rite to pray for a quick recovery or peace and reconciliation, usually on an autumn evening. The people pray, beat drums, slaughter and offer the blood of sacrificial animals, light nine bonfires on the top of a hill, and pile up eighty-one *huochi* (火池, braziers), along with stone and earthen jars and earth around the fires. The *mukūnda* then announces to the deities the reasons for offering their prayers. If the fire flames up and sparks fly upwards, it means that all deities in the wilds and the whole universe give a sign that they have heard the prayers. People perform fire acrobatics and use fire to shape a fire dragon, tiger, python, horse, fish, mountain, and so on. All the clanspeople join the fire teams in celebrating the ritual, and the atmosphere is quite animated. If the wind is too strong, however, it can cause fire or other calamities, so there are quite a number of taboos regarding the rite. The worship of the fire god and other deities is shrouded in mystery, and only if the fire god and the East Sea (Donghai) goddess are invited together, maintaining a balance between fire and water, can the ritual be accomplished smoothly and successfully. Thus, divination and prayer before the rite is vital.

When it has been decided that a fire rite will be held, a clan meeting is normally held to elect the *mukūnda* and *shamanda* (head shaman) in charge of the proceedings. In early spring, the clan then prepares offerings and ritual instruments, stores badger and boar fat in a cellar for oil lamps, and preserves boars, roe deer, swans, pheasants, fish, hazel grouses, wild fruit, and other food for use in the autumn celebration. For the immediate preparations, the *shamanda* leads the clanspeople to put up a thatched hut on a high and tranquil hill, where the clan shamans who will participate in the rite will live. It is forbidden for them to bathe, rest, or go back to their clan for sexual activity. An elder shaman leads them in learning the sacred texts and preparing the ritual utensils. The texts are enshrined in the hut with statuettes of the deities, and two magpies and two male pheasants are caught and kept in a cage. When everything has been prepared and the sacred mountain and sacred tree have been chosen, the site for the sacrifice is divined by a ritual in which people toss a fish tooth in the air and observe where it points. Through further divination, the shaman locates the sacred tree from among the numerous forest trees in the direction indicated. For this purpose, the head elder shaman dresses in their ritual garb, puts on their sacred hat, fastens their waist bells, and begins beating their drum. The other shamans kneel, and the *mukūnda* sprinkles wine and blood and then prays. The elder shaman performs a trance dance, beats their drum, and intones a chant in the forest. Suddenly the drumbeat becomes louder and more intense, and the shaman faints and falls on the ground, lying on their back, unconscious. The tree that rustles above them is taken as the sacred tree for the rite. All the shamans then beat their drums, kneel, and pray. The elder shaman revives, and the procedure for choosing the tree has been completed. Regardless of its size or girth, it is believed to be able to establish communication with heaven and to be the habitat of deities of the universe and clan ancestor deities.

The sacred tree must be an elm or willow, and if the shaman faints under another kind of tree, the shaman has to choose again, which seldom happens. I have never seen such a situation. The shaman's success in identifying precisely the right tree with their eyes shut is interpreted as divine guidance. People regard the ability to do so as shrouded in mystery, but because of experience, shamans have an instinct for identifying the proper tree.

Once the tree and site have been pinned down, people from all around hitch their horse to a cart and head to the site, where they put up thatched huts or animal-hide tents to live and eat in the presence of the sacred tree during the three- to seven-night fire ritual. They determine their camping site by releasing pheasants to see where they land. The undulating terrain and gullies around the sacred tree often make it difficult for the various clan groups to choose their campsite near it and autumn fires, so they use the pheasants to allocate auspicious campsites. The *mukūnda* selects a beautiful, slightly hobbling wild pheasant cock, and people of the various *mukūn* separately kneel to the sacred tree. The representative of the first *mukūn* initiates the release of the pheasant, and the *mukūnda* completes the release. The place where the pheasant perches is marked with the totem flag of that *mukūn*. Subsequently, representatives of the other *mukūn* in turn release their pheasants to determine their campsite. If a pheasant perches in the same area as has already been allotted, a different campsite needs to be located. Once the campsites have been determined, the various groups start to cut wood and build shacks or treehouses or put up tents at their respective sites.

According to the manuscript account of the fire rite as performed by the Seven Hulun Clans, a pine gate is usually built in front of the sacred tree, with four totem poles on each side, on which there are various carved animals and human and animal sketches. Eight flags of totem animals are set in front of the tree: eagle, flying tiger, python, bear, boar, hedgehog, whale, and leopard. People hang numerous charms and fetishes from hunted animals on the tree, hoping that future hunting will be fruitful, and some hang human-shaped spirit idols to pray for longevity and well-being. People also hang cages of magpies and sparrows on the tree, to be released after the ritual has been completed in order to pass on the good news to heavenly deities. The sacrificial offerings themselves are abundant. Apart from those provided by various *mukūn*, there are live boars, wild deer, and hazel grouses provided by the whole clan. A long ditch is filled with fresh water, and in it swim large carp, grass carp, and mandarin dragonet fish. Piles of azalea are set aflame to make azalea *nianxi* incense.[9] The offerings also include roasted suckling pigs, deer breasts, and all kinds of cakes.

Soon afterwards, on a star-filled night, people begin to set out offerings, and at dawn, they begin the rite. To the blare of horns, the *mukūnda* and *shamanda* lead the heads of the various *mukūn* to the sacred tree, followed by shamans leading the clanspeople. As they process forwards, they kneel, beat their drums and a big bass drum, ring bells, and sound *ciyalaci* (wood clappers), creating a huge din. After they kneel, shamans begin the summoning of the gods. Live deer and boar are slaughtered, and their blood is poured into a sacred container, mixed with water, and spread around the sacred tree and over the campground of the various groups. One cup of blood is kept aside by the *mukūnda* to worship the fire god at night. In the afternoon, shamans of the various *mukūn* perform the *bao* ritual of thanksgiving and conduct prayers. After dark, the Big Dipper Nadan Usiha (*nadan* "seven"; *usiha* "stars") rises in the east, and when its head starts pointing towards the western sky, the drums and horns all blare to mark the formal commencement of the fire sacrifice. All the clanspeople are elated.

First, shamans light the bonfires in front of the sacred tree and various oil lamps before the altar, including a beast-head lamp, frog lamp, eagle lamp, leopard lamp, turtle lamp, and fish lamp. Tolon (torches) are lit from the fire, and amid a dancing sea of fire, the *shamanda* intones the chant to raise the fire. The clanspeople echo the chant, enlivening the celebration:

> *Siran tolon mbi – siran tolon* (endless rolling torches, the endless torches)
> *Amba tolon mbi – amba tolon* (huge torches, the huge torches)
> *Usiha tolon mbi – usiha tolon* (starlike torches, torches like stars)
> *Hada tolon mbi – hada tolon* (peak-like torches, torches like peaks)
> *Bira tolon mbi – bila tolon* (river-like torches, torches like rivers)
> *Alin tolon mbi – alin tolon* (mountainous torches, torches like mountains)
> *Mama tolon mbi – mama tolon* (the grandma torches, torches like grandmas)
> *Mama tolon – tolon mama* (grandma, like grandmas)
> *Tolon – tolon – ere* (torches, these torches)
> *Tolon – tolon* (torches, torches)
> *To – lon – ere* (the torches here)
> *To – lon – ere* (the torches here)

According to the Hulun Hala account, during the chant, hundreds of torches made of badger and boar fat are set aflame, illuminating the dark night, and according to other scattered materials that I found, the rite is traditionally performed in similar fashion in the Mengjeje, Kūyala, and Tukri halas. They all light up nine bonfires after the torches are set aflame, and the clan head and his clanspeople worship the stars, the sacred tree, and the fires, which are heaped up with wood and branches in a pyramidal shape and tended by appointed men.

In the rite of the seven Hulun Hala, the bonfires are made into various shapes: some like pythons flying over the mountain, some like crouching tigers, some like galloping horses. The *mukūnda* and *shamanda* design and carefully lay out the fire formations, and clanspeople ride their horses or walk through them in small groups. Only the bravest and cleverest horse riders and hunters can handle the "Fire of Heaven" and pass through the formations safe and sound. They do so to "burn away" evils, believing that only the pure sacred fire can get rid of evil spirits and bring health and good fortune. The one who passes through the fire most often with tact and speed is revered as *baturu* (hero) and elected as the *lieda* (hunting leader) of the clan. The more adroitly they pass through it, the more mystical they become. Their ability has been proven, and they are shown to be protected by the gods and one of auspicious good fortune.

Among the games enjoyed during the celebration are playing hide and seek around the fires, chasing a running hare around them with a stick, tying up a deer or shooting a duck in the fire, and snatching from the fire stone beads, stone cups, and sheep or goat *galaha* (ankle bones used for divination). There are also activities such as going through a loop of fire on a swing, kicking a lantern, and competing in distinctive fire feats on horseback. The whole celebration expresses praise to the invincible power of fire while displaying *mukūn* skills handed down from generations in building, understanding, storing, handling, and fending off fire.

After the games and the accompanying din of wild blasts of trumpets and horns, all the clanspeople gather again in front of the sacred tree, and the shamans beat their drums to invite the deities to share in the joy. To the sound of bell ringing and drumbeats, the eagle god, bear god, and python god descend upon the earth, and the shamans perform stunts of various animal deities in front of the fire. Subsequently, they summon the East Sea goddess Dergiomo Mama, the mother goddess of brightness of the east and life. Pictured as having the head of a fish and a human body, she is worshipped by the Manchu and other northern peoples in line with their reverence of the east as the direction of life, brightness, and hope and her dwelling place. She comes, beating her sacred oval drum, waving ribbons of seven colours, and spraying clear water from her lips. It is thought that only once she has descended upon the earth will the sacrificial fire remain burning without causing damage to humans, beasts, and the forests. In the Manchu creation myth "War in Heaven," depicting the battle between Abka Hehe and the demon Yeluli, the East Sea goddess prevailed against the fire-leopard goddess Tuwa Yarha, and from then on, only the water of the East Sea was able to put out mountain fires. When people want to do so, they first have to piously worship the East Sea goddess. During the fire ritual, only once she has descended can the roaring fire-leopard goddess come, who endows the shamans and clanspeople with skills of handling fire. Then everyone can jump, dance, and perform the *tiaohuochi* feat of running over burning coals uninjured as an auspicious sign or test of divine judgement. As the clanspeople sing the fire song and perform the fire dance, the celebration reaches its climax.

Running the *tiaohuochi* is common among the Manchu and other northern peoples and among religious zealots all over the world. Sri Lankan spirit mediums swiftly run nude across a stone fire-ground heated to a high temperature, and devotees in South Africa and India also worship fire and practise walking on fire. In shamanism, the technique is viewed as mysterious, but it can be scientifically explained. When people run swiftly over a fire that has already been trodden down, their feet stay on the fire for such a short stretch of time that it cannot penetrate the skin. Because the possibility of getting hurt is really not great, people readily run across a blazing fire to seek acclaim. On the whole, fire rituals have played an important role in primitive religious activities, and their widespread popularity serves as evidence that humans had already conquered and freely handled fire in the distant past.

At the end of the Manchu fire rite, all throw their offerings into the bonfires and then pick out burning coals to preserve in small jars, pots, or basins as an "eternal flame." They dismantle their tents, pack up their food and utensils, say goodbye to one another, and go back to their respective *mukūn*, singing and dancing. Except for people who served as guards or were suffering from serious illness, everyone would attend the rite. Men and women, old and young, all become elated, and any hardship, hostility or hatred among clans or *mukūn* would be reconciled under the protection of the sacred tree. They bring the burning coals back to their villages, put them in the hearth or a brazier, and tend the fire well to keep it from dying out. For the next fire rite, sparks from it are brought to a new location and rekindled.

The shamanic texts chanted in the fire ritual are especially beautiful from a literary and artistic point of view and full of mythic meaning. However, many of the texts were neglected or forgotten by Manchu ancestors and so gradually got scattered and disappeared. Many such texts have become nothing but the monotonous, ossified chants heard in temples or shrines – an irreparable loss for the study of the northern cultures of China. The existing material available to scholars is but a drop in the bucket.

Notes

1 Jiuli 九黎: Each tribe was imagined as having nine subtribes, led by a total of eighty-one brother chieftains. Later, the legendary Emperor Yan 炎帝 and Emperor Huang 黄帝 are said to have allied against Chiyou at Zhuoluv 涿鹿, present-day Hebei, and defeated him.

2 The *Book of Rites* 《礼记》 is a collection of texts describing the social forms, administration, and rites of the Zhou dynasty, Warring States Period (475–221 BCE), and early Han period (206 BCE–220 CE)

3 Such documents include *Records of Sacrificial Rules and Procedures of the Fu Clan* (*Fushi jigui chengxu lixulu*), *Uyun Divine Words of the Qian Clan* (*Qianxing wuyun shenyu*), and *Norms for Sacrificial Rites of the Zang Clan* (*Dazang dingshi shenji guiyi*). In addition, the elderly Oroqen shaman Mo Fusheng had in his possession *Hundred Divine Words* (*Buju shenyu*), and the Daur shaman Wu Dekun had *Kunhe Esoteric Divine Words* (*Kunhe shoushen mizhuan zunyu*).

4 The *Sierranju* is a traditional Ewenki dwelling, covered in the summer with birch bark and in the winter with deer furs. It has a conical shape, is constructed from twenty to thirty pine poles, and is usually about 6 metres in diameter and 5 metres in height.

5 *Rites of Zhou* first appeared in a 2nd century BCE collection of old texts.

6 The Five Great Mountains 五岳 were famous mountains that were imperial ritual sites: East Great Mountain *Tai Shan*泰山, West Great Mountain Hua Shan华山, South Great Mountain Heng Shan 衡山 in Hunan, North Great Mountain Heng Shan 恒山, and Centre Great Mountain Song Shan嵩山.

7 Yellow Hat Sect (Huangjiao黄教); isthe popular Mongolian name for Buddhism originating from the Tibetan Gelugpa sect, whose monks wear a yellow hat while performing religious services.

8 *Khata* is a Tibetan Buddhist ritual swath of silk symbolizing purity and compassion and worn or presented with incense on ceremonial occasions. Mongolian *khatas* are usually blue, symbolizing the sky, and are commonly tied to *ovoo*, stupas, or sacred trees and stones.

9 *Nianxi* incense 年息香 is a Manchu ritual incense made from azaleas picked before July 7 of the lunar year, dried naturally under the sun, and then ground into powder.

5 Rituals for nature deities

Chapter 2 discussed aspects of the northern shamanic worship of nature: heavenly phenomena, fire, earth, water, birds, and so on. The present chapter describes several of the rituals commonly used in worshipping nature gods, in particular star, sea, willow, bear, and snake deities.

5.1 Star rituals

In Chapter 2, we stated that the northern shamanic worship of the sky or heaven includes the sun, moon, stars, and all natural phenomena associated with the sky. According to *Records of Four Manchu Rites* (*Manzhou siliji*), such heavenly phenomena are called *shen* (神, deities), while those of the earth are called *qi* (祇, earth deities), but in general, the whole system is referred to as the worship of heaven (*tian*, 天). Ancient as rites worshipping heaven, they came into prominence later than blood and fire rites.

Rituals worshipping the stars are an integral part of the worship of heaven, and for ages, they have been one of the most influential practices observed by Manchu and other northern peoples. When people moved from the barbaric period to tribal society, they experienced a relatively stable stage of life and livelihood, and they came to have a clearer sense of geographical relationships and concepts. They began to take interest in noting the positions and alterations of the stars and formulating laws that govern them, and they associated the stars and their movements with their own lives and religious beliefs. The heavens were thus no longer isolated entities bearing no relationship to human beings; they were seen as mystical messengers and helpful forces for whom humans yearned and on whom humans depended. They were included in the ranks of shamanic deities and came to have their own rituals. Although star rituals came into being at a later stage in northern peoples' religious development than blood rituals and fire rituals, they became more and more dynamic and vital with the development of society. Many pious believers found it exceedingly interesting to explore the heavens, and star rituals came to have great appeal. Even now, star rites arguably influence the daily life of northern ethnic peoples.

As we have seen, the influence of Manchu and Mongol cultures has been stronger than that of other northern peoples in the region. They absorbed, moreover, more Han cultural elements than did other ethnic groups, such as the practice recorded in the 2nd-century BCE *Rites of Zhou* (*Zhouli*) of offering fire sacrifices to the sun, moon, and stars. *Old Jilin Records* (*Jilin jiuwenlu*) states that among the many Manchu sacrificial rituals, star rites and ancestor rites were equally important, and *Annals of Jilin* (*Jilin tongzhi*) records that among all northern rituals, the Manchu star and ancestor rituals were the grandest. They were held once a year or several years and demanded great expense. Star rites were far more important among the Manchu than they were in other ethnic groups, and they bore a close resemblance to Han Chinese practices. Of Han practices, *Rules for Manchu Sacrifices to Deities and Heaven* (*Qinding manzhou jitian jishen dianli*) recounts that from the reign of Emperor Qianlong (乾隆, 1735–1799), sacrificial rites should conform to the long-standing rules of the past, and from the numerous instances of shamanic star worship of Manchu clans, we can get glimpses into the basic features of ancient Manchu star rituals.

The ancient Manchu observed the stars in their particular geographical locations in the north for generations. They catalogued cyclical phenomena such as the rise and setting of the sun and moon; the orbits of Venus, Jupiter, Mercury, Mars, and Saturn; the positions of stars; and the shapes, numbers, luminosity, and metamorphoses of the constellations. On the basis of the yearly appearance of the constellations, or "mansions" (*xiu*, 宿) in the northern sky, people predicted seasonal climate changes, the direction and force of winds, the exact time of solar events, and possible temperature ranges and variations. They did so in accord with their understanding of both heavenly phenomena themselves and the modes of life and migration patterns of various animals and the estimated yield of plants and herbs. They observed the sun, moon, and stars to predict weather conditions for the coming year, and they recognized that various changes in nature correspond to constellations in the same area and predicted the weal and woe of the clan accordingly. At the same time, their observations of the heavens inspired their unique star rituals, which took shape in patriarchal society before shamanist ancestor worship emerged.

The Mongols have also had long deep reverence for the stars, especially for the Big Dipper, to which they would offer kumis and animal sacrifice. Nonetheless, they revered the sun and the moon even more. The Tartars, as the Mongol invaders where known to Europeans,

> worshipped the sun, the moon, mountains and rivers and the five planets. The doors of their yurts were built to face the south, before which they would kneel down to worship the sun, pouring wine onto the ground. When they worshipped the sun, the moon, the mountains, the rivers, or the various celestial bodies, they would sprinkle liquor on the ground.

Mongol herders worshipped the sky out of the need for a greater abundance of flocks. A scene of such worship is inscribed on the rock paintings on the Yin Mountains of Inner Mongolia; the paintings were carved by the Hun nomads who dominated the Asian Steppe from the 3rd century BCE to the late 1st century CE and by the proto-Mongolian nomadic Xianbei people, the Mongols themselves, and other ethnic peoples. The paintings depict the sun, the moon, the stars, and clouds with scenes of people worshipping the sun or dancing to the stars (Li Di 1986:16).

The Oroqen also had a grasp of meteorological knowledge. They traditionally recognized that if stars twinkled at night, there would be high winds the following day; if the sun rose with *dair* (bright spots on its sides called sun dogs), it would be warm that day; if the sun set with *dair*, it would be cold the following day; if there was a halo on either side of the moon, it would also be cold the following day; and so on. They did not traditionally choose auspicious days for weddings, funerals, and sacrificial rites according to an almanac; they did so by observing the waxing and waning of the moon. The Ewenki used the sun and the constellation of the Three Stars (Shen Xiu, 参宿) to tell time (Li Di 1986:16), and when they travelled at night, their only compass was the Three Stars and Big Dipper. To predict the coming year, they observed the position of the moon and the Chinese Southern Dipper. If the moon was at the upper left of the Dipper, there would be floods in the coming year; if it was at the upper right, there would be drought; and if it lay within or under the Dipper, there would be a good harvest with adequate rainfall and moderate temperature. The Manchu, like their Jurchen ancestors, still tell time according to the positions of stars. If the sky is overcast with no bright stars, they decide time on the basis of dimmer stars.

The original geographical scope of activity of northern ethnic groups was mainly between the thirty-sixth degree and the fiftieth degree of north latitude. Some groups had to go far up to the sub-frigid zones of the north to seek a living by fishing and hunting. The periods when the land was covered with ice and snow in these zones lasted longer than nine months, with long winter nights and short summers. Sometimes people had to live in the snow under the stars, and faced with such harsh conditions, they longed for light and fire, which could expel evil and cold and allow them to live and reproduce. This is likely the core motivation for early shaman star rituals in the region.

The stars worshipped in early shamanism were the winter constellations (mansions) in the northern hemisphere known as the "winter stars" (*jilengxing*, 祭冷星) or the "night stars" (*jiyexing*,祭夜星), which were considered to be the dwelling place of deities in charge of night and cold. There were also the Manchu fire goddess Tuwa Enduri, with her sun horse Šūn Morin; Weledū Mama, the goddess who lays out the stars; and the mama goddesses who taught humans life skills. Among the terms used in star rites ("star," *usiha* in Manchu) are *tumen usiha* (ten thousand stars), *mingan usiha* (one thousand stars), and *oron weceku* (star shrine niche). It was believed that the numerous cloudlike constellations were a dynamic world with life, spirit, consciousness, cognition, human character, and pathos. The stars were harmonious as equal members of the huge family of the heavens, bustling like humans day and night but possessing transcendental divine power. They are like birds flying in the sky with the luminous brilliance of their feathers, so shaman chants call them *wedun gasha* (birds of the universe), *aisin gasha* (golden birds), and *menggun gasha* (silver birds). They fly in orderly formations from east to west with their glittering white wings day and night. They chase the sun god during the day and the moon god at night, casting a lustrous silver glow upon the earth. The brilliant sun, the tender luminous moon, and the twinkling stars have been deeply revered and exalted as the eyes of heaven. People thought that white was the true colour of the universe, as well as of the sun, the moon, starlight, and flames, and they revered it as the colour not only of the heavens but also of purity, life, and good fortune. In general, they regarded white as the symbol of youth, yellow as the symbol of the prime of life, and red as a sign of decline and foreboding pointing to life's twilight.

Among the various deities worshipped in the night *beideng* rite with all lights out, mentioned in Chapter 3, there is the great goddess in charge of setting out the stars in the universe, Weledū Mama, mother of the heavens, one of the three sisters of the universe in the Manchu creation myth "War in Heaven." With a human body and a pair of bird's wings, she is usually dressed in a fur gown with white feathers and is seen as carrying a small fur sack full of stars on her back. In the *beideng* rite, a shaman dressed in a white gown shakes their waist bells and flaps their arms to symbolize the flight of the goddess in the sky as they chant a sacred text. The shaman's soul thus ascends to the nine-storey heaven to visit the deities of the universe, animal deities, and clan ancestor deities. While doing so, the shaman prays for Weledū Mama's aid, hoping that she will give the shaman white wings, make the twinkling stars guide them by illuminating their way, guard them, provide them with food and water, or lend to his soul the Star Bridge as a resting place on this long journey. In the Manchu tale "Sirin Sefu," when the shaman Sirin visited heaven, it took him ten days in a trance to get to the Golden Mansion, where the East Sea goddess Aomu Mama lives. In any case, a shaman's soul cannot soar to the heavens without the help of star deities. In the Manchu *Jiao'uyun* training programme for shaman initiates and other ritual activities, chants to praise and worship the stars are performed with great reverence, and star rites are quite complicated and have rigid taboos. Among northern peoples, the Manchu possess the most documented records of star rituals. As can be seen in *Records of Grievances of the East Sea* (*Donghai chenyualu*) and other Manchu folk materials, the ancient Jurchen of the Donghai Weji (forest) tribe worshipped the stars twice a year, either separately or together with the worship of their ancestors. When people worshipped the stars right after the first snow, they hoped that they could have abundant food for winter, and when they worshipped them in the first month of the lunar year (solar February), they hoped to dispel evils, banes, and plagues and prayed for peace and health for the new year.

The star rite at the first snow was held when there rose up in the eastern sky the constellation Nehu Usiha (Pleiades or Seven Sisters, in Chinese lore Maoxiu). During this ritual, nine piles of long logs are set aflame as horns and drums blare. The nine clouds of smoke belching from the blazing bonfires are like nine columns billowing up to the heaven as the Star Bridge. The smoke columns "connect the sacred tree with heaven," and the fires expel evil and illuminate the world while protecting the star deities from evil spirits so that they can stay bright every night, guide people on earth, and deliver good news. The star ritual of the first lunar month traditionally included the nine bonfires and sacrifices of deer, boars, wild geese, pheasants, and other wild animals. The whole animal was not necessarily offered, but when it was still alive, its blood was sprinkled in the woods and on the fires, and some of its flesh was roasted and offered in sacrifice. Wooden bowls and grass stalks were used as dishes and utensils, which illustrates the way of eating in Manchu *ye* rituals held to worship nature deities.

The grand star ritual cited in *Longjiang Annals* (*Longjiang xianzhi*) goes as follows: at night, people worship the stars in front of the chimney of the east house, with the lights out. When the rite begins, a person dressed in white kneels on the ground, holding a wooden knife in their left hand. They stab a pig, offers sacrifice, and then, with their relatives, eats the meat (Longjiang Annals Editorial Committee 1991). *Etiquette and Customs of Hulan Banner* (*Hulan difangqiji lisu*) from the reign of Emperor Guangxu (1875–1908) states the same: the Manchu of the Hulan District of Harbin worship stars at night in front of the east chimney of the principal house, with the lights out. A person dressed in white kneels, prays, and slays a pig with a knife in their left hand. Of the rite of the Kūyala Hala (clan), the star ritual is held on the night of an auspicious day after the three-day spring ploughing ritual (*Chungengji*, 春耕祭), when stars are neatly distributed throughout the sky. People set up an altar at the west of the house towards the Big Dipper and prepare a willow branch on which seven chicken wing feathers are bound with thin hemp. For the Irgen Gioro Hala of Ula, Jilin Province, the pig sacrificed in the star ritual should weigh under 50 *jin* (1 *jin* is equivalent to 0.5 kilograms); regardless of its weight, it must be carried by two people into the west chamber of the principal house and laid on bare ground with its head turned to the northeast. People set up ancestor tablets on a long altar table and invite the ancestors to enjoy the celebration together with the star gods. To pray for peace and health, they poor liquor into the pig's left ear. In a procedure known as *lingsheng* (领牲, sacrificial animal), if the ear twitches, that means that the god has accepted the offering. Also required are seven stacks of seven flat buckwheat cakes in the shape of the Big Dipper. Cups are filled with liquor, and seven pairs of chopsticks made of sorghum stalks are stood upright beside the cake stacks.

As I found in my field trips in Heilongjiang, Jilin, and other areas, Manchu star rituals continue to follow these old customs. The shamans are mostly dressed in white, but for some clans in yellow; the sacrificial animals are mostly piglets and birds; the number of offerings is three, seven, or nine (an odd number). The utensils used at the sacrificial meal are made of wood or sorghum stalks, but not chopsticks; the firewood consists of pine torches or candles, not bonfires. In some families, the rite is simplified and subsumed under the *jia* ritual (*jiaji*, 家祭), as was noted in Chapter 3. The form of shaman rites were standardized in the mid-Qing era without spirit possession and were not necessarily a family rite, though *jia* basically means house or home. When the star gods are worshipped as a part of the night *beideng* ritual, the rite is similarly simplified, by omitting the sacred chants praising the stars. In 1980, I went to in Jilin Province and visited the expert of Manchu folklore Zhao Jinwen (赵金文), Manchu elders,[1] and an elderly woman named Luo, all of whom recalled the details of the rite as performed in

Ula. They all stated that the tradition of reverencing the stars among the Manchu, old and young alike, has been an established practice handed down for ages to remind later generations of the hardships of the early settlements in the area. The shaman and clan chieftain would lead the clan to worship the stars in the traditional way, and anyone who violated the taboos was severely punished, with no exception.

Located 40 *li* (1 *li* is equivalent to 0.5 kilometres) northeast of the town of Ula is the famous Phoenix Mountain (Fenghuangshan), on which there were once many old temples. From the reign of Kangxi (康熙) until that of Qianlong (乾隆), 1661–1796, the Manchu villages near the mountain had the tradition of worshipping stars. When a star rite was held, numerous bonfires blazed on its crest and slopes all night long, like a stretch of bright stars. During the rite, shamans of various clans would gather to elect the clan to take charge of the rite in accordance with the tradition that people of the same tribe would worship the stars together in the same way. The fleece of white sheep, horse hides, and rabbit fur could all be used to make the ritual garb, worn with the fleece or fur on the outside. Shamans were stationed at different spots on the mountain, where they would beat their drums and chant a hymn to the stars, and all the people would sing a choral anthem that could be heard for miles around.

When people worshipped the stars, they had to call out to them. The more frequently they called, the brighter the stars would become, and this was believed to keep the stars free from harm and evil spirits. People had to prepare sacrificial animals; cast their blood and flesh, along with grains and rice wine, into the fire; and then build a fireplace with white stones as a temporary hearth to roast the meat. After the rite, all of the tribe would assemble around rows of wooden troughs, dip their hands in salt water, and together eat the meat roasted over the "fire of heaven." Although the rite was commonly held in the dead of winter, the scene was quite spectacular. Some clans or families would hold the ritual separately at other times for particular purposes but according to the same procedure. According to anthropological studies, women were not allowed to take part in the ritual. In fact, however, the Manchu and other northern peoples were not much influenced by Confucianism. Women could ride horses or sleighs to join in the worship of the stars and pray for blessings. If there were passing travellers of other tribes, moreover, they were warmly welcomed as distinguished guests to enjoy the sacrificial meal together with the clanspeople. Actually, people believed that they would bring good luck and that the greater number people who attended the rite, the more neatly would the Stars appear and the more prosperous would the coming year turn out to be.

During the rite, clanspeople would have competitions of fire skills and games, such as jumping through "dragon fire hoops," forming fire formations, swinging bundles of fire, horse riding, and shooting. From the middle of the Qing dynasty onwards, all kinds of fireworks displays and radiant fire shows flourished. People made a star observation platform out of snow and ice like a silver tower on the top of the mountain, and they fashioned on the mountain top with sacred animals and birds out of snow, which appeared like deities descending in luminous fire. If snakes were seen crawling out of stone caverns during the rite, this was regarded as an auspicious sign, and people took care not to step on them or kill them. The shamans and clanspeople would then stir up the bonfires more brightly, slaughter animals, offer the animals' blood, and give thanks to heaven, shouting "A huge snake is coming; spring is approaching."

Star rites are still talked about not only by the Manchu but by other northern peoples as well. Ancient documents record that other northern fishing and hunting peoples have long had star rituals. *Book of Later Han Vol. 8* (*Houhanshu*, 445 CE), relates that the ancient Korean kingdom of Goguryeo (37 BCE–668 CE) liked to build shrines to worship the stars and also gods of the soil and grain. Many documents describe northern customs in the days of the Liao and Great Jin dynasties, of worshipping the stars and heaven, of regarding birds as star gods, and of predicting weather conditions in accordance with movements of the heavens and stars.

The shamanic custom of Shunxing (顺星), worship of the star deity in charge of the current year of the sixty-year Chinese calendrical cycle, has prevailed in northern China for hundreds of years. Shunxing originally focused on worshipping Taisui (太岁), the stars opposite the planet Jupiter, dating back to the 11th-century BCE Shang dynasty, and the use of the sixty-year cycle itself can be found in the 3rd-century BCE Zhou dynasty. When the mother of Jin Emperor Zhangzong (章宗, 1189–1209) fell ill for a long time, she soon recovered when the emperor prayed to the current year's deity Dingmao (丁卯) and built a shrine to house the god's statue. The custom of Shunxing grew more popular in the Yuan dynasty (1279–1368), and Ming Emperor Yongle (永乐, 1360–1424) issued an edict for the construction in Beijing of the White Cloud Temple (*Baiyunguan*), which was called Auspicious Sign Temple (*Yuancheng-dian*) in the Qing years and known by the common people as Shunxing Temple (*Shunxingdian*).

Regarding Beijing rites worshipping the stars, the 1937*Collected Customs of Beiping* (*Beiping fengsu leizheng*) records a legend: on the eighth day of the first month of the lunar year, all the star deities would descend to earth, and people would light lanterns to worship them. They could light up as many as 108 lanterns, but they lit forty-nine as the common practice. People also worshipped the star gods of their birth year and offered them star-shaped *yuanxiao* (元宵, glutinous rice balls). They would give the *yuanxiao* to relatives and friends as a present until the lantern lights began to dim (Li Jiarui 1992). *Records of Seasonal Yanjing Customs* (*Yanjing suishiji*) by the Qing standard-bearer Dun Lichen at the beginning of the 20th century contains a record of the same rite (Yanjing 燕京, another old name for Beijing). After dusk on the eighth day of the first month of the lunar year, people lit 108 lanterns with oil mixed with wine and burnt incense to send tribute to the stars in what was known as the star ritual. From the thirteenth to the sixteenth day of the first lunar month, people hung and lit flower-shaped paper lanterns called *sandenghua* (散灯花) in their rooms and the house hall, all the way to the gate, to get rid of evil (Pan Rongbi 1981).

Since 12th-century Jin dynasty times, this custom has been popular in the northern areas of China above the Yangtze River. Some scholars claim that it should be attributed to the spread of Taoism ever since the Han dynasty (206 BCE–220 CE), which traditionally worshipped goddesses in charge of stars, the heavens, mountains, and rivers, and the soil goddess Houtu (后土). However, Yanjing (Beijing) culture was also deeply influenced by Jurchen culture, and the content and structure of the star rite of the White Cloud Temple conforms more to the Manchu shaman Shunxing's star worship. The influence of ancient Han culture and Taoism may have added to the complexity of the Beijing star rite, but its roots lie rather in shamanism. In any case, the shaman chants and oracles that I have known among northern peoples have become mingled over time with the Beijing star ritual ever since the Han dynasty two thousand years ago.

On the other side of the coin, elements of traditional Chinese astronomical lore have become mingled over the ages with the star rituals performed among the Manchu and other peoples. Ancient Chinese astronomers divided the sky into four regions, collectively known as the four symbols, and they assigned to each a mystic animal: azure dragon of the east, black tortoise of the north, white tiger of the west, and vermilion bird of the south. Each region contains seven mansions, in total twenty-eight, which were determined in the spring and autumn and the Warring States Period (475–221 BCE) of the Zhou dynasty. These mansions are the equivalent of the Western zodiac constellations, but they are based on the movement of the moon through a sidereal month, not that of the sun in a tropical year.

When did the Twenty-Eight Mansions and other imperial astrological concepts begin to appear among northern ethnic peoples? On the basis of archaeological findings, we know that this happened at least as early as the Liao dynasty (916–1125). The Liao star chart found in the 1970s in Zhangjiakou, Hebei, is one of the most significant archaeological findings in the astronomical history of northern China. The chart is based mainly on the Twenty-Eight Mansions of China, along with the twelve Babylonian signs of the zodiac. It was the first such chart found in China that includes foreign astronomical references. The late-12th-century *Compilation of Documents of The Three Reigns' Northern Alliance* (*Sanchao Beimeng Huibian*), concerning the reigns of the first three Great Jin emperors, records that in the Jin dynasty (1115–1234), "archery competitions were organized among Jurchen clans and the titles of officials were named after the Palace of Nine Stars and Twenty-Eight Mansions" (Xu Mengshen 1987). From this, we can surmise that the astronomical concept of the Twenty-Eight Mansions was well known in Manchu households and that the deities of the Twenty-Eight Mansions were then revered in shaman chants.

On the basis of years of field study, interviews with shamans, and shamanic texts, we have found that the astronomical system of northern peoples was enriched during the evolution of society and gradually took shape as star rituals. From this, we can deduce that the embryo of the Manchu system actually appeared much earlier than did the Twenty-Eight Mansions of the Zhou dynasty. The Manchu system emerged earlier, moreover, than the twelve signs of the Western zodiac, the constellations, and mythological map of the sky that has long been in use worldwide. The ancient star names, attributes, positions, and customs preserved in Manchu shamanism were cultivated according to the stars as seen in autumn, winter, and spring in northern China. Observation of these stars allowed people to identify changes in seasons, geographical positions, the time of day, and climate.

Nadan Nalahū was the leading star goddess in the eastern sky and assistant to the goddess Weledū Mama in her duty of setting out the stars. She is sometimes called Nalahū, Nahū, or Nadan Daihūn, and her mansion is also known as Chicken Nest (*jiwoxing*), Umbrella (*sanzixing*), Flower Bud (*huagutuoxing*), Seven Sisters (*qizimeixing*), and Seven Fairies (*qixiannv*). Some think her mansion refers to the Big Dipper, but the Big Dipper is Nadan Usiha (Seven Stars), which is worshipped separately in the *beideng* rite but together with Ilan Usiha (Three Stars) in the star rite.

According to ancient northern folklore, the light and fire of life dwells in the East, where the sun, moon, and stars rise. People had the custom of worshipping the sun and kneeling towards it out of their recognition that its changes are intimately related to the geographical conditions in which they lived. They regarded the northern sky where the sun, moon, and stars always rose in the east and set in the west as the most sacred place, and they imagined that the two goddesses Nalahū and Weledū Mama enjoyed playing in the heavens and occasionally liked to conceal the starlight under their feathered dresses, plunging the sky into complete darkness. Consequently, when shamans worshipped stars, they loudly chanted "words to awaken the stars." Nadan Nalahū was at the centre of all the stars in winter, and as winter moved into the spring, the two goddesses led all the stars to rise quietly in the east when the sun set and ordered the mansions to head slowly westwards. When the two sunk in the western sky in winter, the sun began to rise in the east. They were worshipped as the supreme ancestral goddesses. For her part, the seven stars (Big Dipper) goddess Nadan Usiha appeared much later than did the great goddess of the universe Nadan Nalahū Nalahū. She came into being only after agriculture became common and people began to lead settled lives. She was worshipped by kneeling towards the north.

There are many summer stars that usher in the harvest: heart (*xin*), tail (*wei*), neck (*kang*), dustpan (*qi*), and other mansions in the region of the Four Stars in the Room Mansion, which *Book of Han* (*Hanshu*) says care for agriculture. According to the etymological dictionary *Ciyuan*, the stars in the Heart Mansion were called Big Fire (*dahuo*) or Shang Star (shangxing). They were known as the Three Flaming Stars (*resanxing*) among the people and served as the counterpart of the Three Stars Mansion Ilan Usiha in winter because they never appeared with the Three Stars. These agrarian stars are quite different in purpose from the winter stars worshipped in shamanism. Serving purely farming purposes, they were "worshipped to pray for good rain," but "if there was excessive rainfall, people prayed for more sunny days, and if there was drought in winter, people prayed for snow." *Collected Customs of Beiping* adds detail: "The northern people in general believed that when the Three Stars set at daybreak, the river is going to freeze" (Li Jiarui 1992).

Many statements about stars can be found in well-known farming proverbs:

When the Eagle Star [*yingxing*] *sets in the west,*
it will take a long time for the sun to emerge.
A halo around the Mouse Star [*shuxing*] *chills the winds*
and brings freezing torrents.
If the handle of the Big Dipper points north,
it ushers in a wintry season.
If the handle of the Big Dipper points north,
snow will be up to the thighs.
If stars blink their eyes, winds will chill the cheeks.
If starlight is braided, snowflakes will fly unabated.

Other sayings based on heavenly phenomena are:

The autumn equinox puts an end to thunder.
The start of winter drives earthworms into hiding.
The start of winter freezes water.
A major snowfall fells elks' antlers.

All such proverbs express generalizations of northern Chinese peoples on the basis of observations of stars and laws of nature, and they have played important roles in grasping seasonal changes and deciding agricultural matters. In general, the star rituals of northern shamanism constitute a prologue to scientific astronomy in the region and a vital contribution to the development of Chinese astronomy in general.

5.2 Sea rituals

Primarily conducted to worship the goddess of the sea and seek her consent for the succession of a new khan, sea rites usually began at night and lasted until sunrise. The main participants were the chieftains, family heads, and shamans of a particular tribe. Shamans – arms and feet bare – wore costumes made of fish skin, girded themselves with waist bells, and equipped themselves with numerous spirit idols and amulets made of fish bones, clam shells, fish eyes, and stones all over their bodies. After bonfires have been lit and the shamans' bodies have been anointed with fish oil and fish blood, they ride boats or rafts out into the rough sea. Some tribespeople kneel on the beach or cliffs, and others go out into the sea with the shamans on rafts or special sea-dragon boats carved out of wood.

As the din of drumbeats, conch shells, trumpets and other horns resounds in everyone's ears and reaches the sky, the head shaman kneels on the ground and invites the East Sea (Donghai) goddess. The shaman then enquires into whether the goddess agrees with the succession of the new khan, chieftain, or tribal head. For a new khanum, the shaman cuts her hair, draws blood from her forehead, and sprinkles the hair and blood into the sea. If no whirlpool-shaped white waves immediately appear, that means that the deity does not recognize the new khanum.

In that case, more blood must be sprinkled as sacrifice into the sea, along with offerings of chickens, ducks, deer, bears, cattle, sheep, or wild boars, which are cast into the sea. If still no white waves are seen, the shaman brings a whale kept in a sea cage, draws blood from it, and drips its blood into the sea. When the waves then turn red, the shaman kneels down again in prayer while the new khanum kneels on one of the rafts, her forehead still bleeding. When silver waves are seen, the whole tribe cheers. It is a sign that the goddess approves the succession, so the new khanum can take charge. She first offers sacrifice, tossing into the sea several virgin boys – not women or male adults. Before sacrificing the boys, she must touch their penises, indicating that the sea goddess should accept the human offerings because they are pure and are the khanum's favourites.

When people pray for a good harvest or a military victory, they perform a similar grand sea rite in which the sacrificial offerings likewise must be males. The rite came to be held among the Donghai Jurchen ancestors of the Manchu in days of matriarchal clan society, when women played a more significant role and men were deemed as just tribal appendages belonging to women. This demonstrates how matriarchal power was then supreme, but aspects of the tradition have been preserved even into modern times.

Still another type of sea ritual has traditionally been held as a burial rite. Manchu clans that sprung from the Donghai Weji tribe tell stories about the ancient burial traditions of people living by the sea, who preferred sea or sky burial to inhumation and cremation. In northern shamanism, human life is a gift from the East Sea goddess, and when people die, their souls should return to the Sea Palace, where the goddess dwells. Therefore, when a tribesperson died, shamans would offer prayers and splice together a raft. The corpse would then be placed at the centre of the raft, surrounded by clothes, commonly used household utensils, and a favourite dog, bird, or other small animal. During the burial rite, shamans beat their drums, ride boats out to the deep sea before the wind rises, and pray for the arrival of the goddess Tasituri, who escorts the dead to the Sea Palace. When possessed by the goddess, the officiating shaman falls into a trance, in which they order the tribespeople and head of the family to steer the raft towards a wind-blown bay or sea regarded as the burial site designated by the goddess. Subsequently, the family head tosses into the sea offerings such as cakes, wild fruit, and the blood of a deer, eagle, or other animal. When silk-like red ripples appear, it means that the seaweed of souls has clustered in the waves. All the boats then gather around the raft bearing the corpse, and the shamans load heavy stones onto raft and then lay them on the corpse, all the while chanting and beating their drums as they pray. When the stones submerge the raft into the depths of the sea, the burial comes to an end. Afterwards, live animal sacrifices are tossed into the sea, and stones are attached to another raft with earthen jars, stone pots, or wooden troughs containing whale and other animal oil. The oil is set aflame, and the boats all set out for the return to land. The light of the flames can sometimes last several days, and when it dies out, the tribespeople believe that the goddess Tasituri has taken the soul of the deceased to the wonderous Sea Palace and that the deceased's loved ones need not to worry anymore.

In modern times, due to the frequent territorial changes, wars, and ethnic migrations since the Qing dynasty (1644–1911), the tradition of the sea ritual has ceased to be practised in many clans. However, it has still been preserved by the Manchu Nimaca Hala and Hexeri Hala, the latter being the oldest clan in Huichun, Jilin Province. He Yulin (何玉霖), an elderly master shaman there who passed away a few years before this book was written was not only familiar with traditional shamanic chants but could recite numerous folk songs. In recollections at his home in the summer of 1982, he said that he knew nothing about sea rituals but that he knew of earlier river rituals from his father and uncle, such as had once been held on the Huichun River to exorcise smallpox. When he recited river ritual chants for us, he referred to the rite as *aomuhe fucembi*, meaning sea ritual, as the name that had been passed down. This shows that, in days gone by, clan ancestors actually held sea rituals. When He Yulin danced as a youth in a shaman *ye* rite, he had once conducted a river ritual in which the otter god was summoned, and he dove into the river to collect shells. But the rite was just a part of the *ye* rite, with no special procedures of its own.

Another Huichun old-timer, the deceased Manchu master shaman Yang Shichang (杨世昌) of the Nimaca Hala from Jiutai County, Jilin, recalled in 1981 that a river ritual had been held at Chaliba Village of Yongji County in the days when he was a newly initiated shaman, to seek respite from a flood. People just killed a pig, offered its blood, roasted the meat over an open fire, and then ate, from which we can see how the ritual had become simplified over time. In river rituals performed as a session of *ye* rites by some clans, people would summon the waterfowl god and otter god and enhance the celebration with winter swimming feats, such as diving and resurfacing through ice holes. From these activities, too, we can see how the sea ritual has undergone drastic changes. Nonetheless, the worship and myths of the East Sea goddess are still preserved in river rituals and other *ye* rituals.

5.3 Willow rituals

In northern shamanism, certain plants were regarded as sacred objects and worshipped as deities, including trees, such as birch, elm, and willow (*fodo* in Manchu). Willows are found primarily in moist soil or on riverbanks, where they are known in northern China as willow swamp stretches and grow rapidly. The Jurchen ancestors of the Manchu lived mainly on fishing and hunting along rivers, and they found willows to be a most useful tree. They used its wood for firewood and making containers. Gradually, moreover, they came to regard willows as deities and created numerous myths and legends that reinforced this belief. Willow worship goes part and parcel with water worship. Northeast China is certainly not wanting in rivers and lakes, but the winters are cold and long. Water is indispensable for life, but drilling wells was more difficult there than in southern China, so people relied on seeking out willows as indicators of a nearby water fountainhead. Willows thus became a symbol of life-giving water, and finding a water supply meant finding the source of life and the foundation of existence and tribal development. Willows and their leaves have thus been regarded as sacred objects and held with great reverence. Whereas the grand fire ritual reflects the pride of conquering the northern world of snow, willow rituals express the delight of finding water and have been celebrated with rapturous enthusiasm among the Manchu, Oroqen, Ewenki, Daur, Xibe, Hezhe, and Mongols. The 1st-century CE literary text *Baihutong* (*A Compilation of Conference Materials on the Confucian Classics in the Eastern Han Dynasty*) recounts that the place where the Tatars inhabited was extremely cold. But a willow survived the cold, and the native people regarded it as an exotic plant and hurried to see it in spring (Ban Gu班固1985). From this, we know that people north of the Gobi Desert long ago regarded willows as sacred plants.

Numerous legends and myths give expression to peoples' belief in the sacredness of the willow. According to a legend recorded in historical documents such as the *Veritable Records of the Manchu* (*Manzhou lu*) from the first half of the 17th century, the celestial maiden Fogulun swallowed a red fruit and thus gave birth to the primogenitor Manchu ancestor Bukūri Yongšon. In one episode of the legend, he went by canoe to suppress a riot in the Jurchen region of Sanxing (present day Yilan, Harbin), and as he was heading down the river to the far shore, he "snapped off a willow branch and bent it to sit on." He was obviously sitting on a willow mat, but the episode suggests that it was sacred. Apparently out of reverence for willows, *History of Jin: Treatise on Geography* (*Jinshi dili zhi*), compiled by 14th-century Mongol historian Toqto'a (also known as Tuotuo), records that in 1165, the fourth year of Jin Emperor Shizong (金世宗), the emperor ordered people to plant willows on both sides of the lane outside the capital gate, stretching for hundreds of *li*. The treatise also says that the Jurchen would reverently place thick willow branches in their *tangse* shrines and use them to punish children and household servants (Toqto'a et al. 1975). In recent times, willows have still lined the countryside lanes of the Shuangcheng District of Harbin, and "baskets and drinking vessels are traditionally made mostly of willow wicker" (Shuangcheng Annals Editorial Committee 1990).

Willow rituals figured prominently in shaman practices and became widespread folk customs. Jurchen in the Liao dynasty used to shoot at willows on the fifth day of the fifth month of the lunar year. In the subsequent Jin dynasty, children would use *fodo* (willows) to sweep tombs on Qingming (Tomb-Sweeping Day), and people would stick willow branches around tombs in worship. *Collected Customs of Beiping* (*Beiping fengsu leizheng*) relates that "On the day of Qingming, women and children would wear willow twigs whose buds were just unfolding like mulberries" and that "people pinned twigs of willow in their hair" (Li Jiarui 1992). According to *Customs of Bukui* (*Bukui fengtu ji*), there was a willow in the southern part of the city that was regarded as a deity and received incense from the local people because they believed its branches could cure disease.

The Oroqen and Ewenki have traditionally revered willows, along with pines, birches, and buckthorns, as sacred. When a senior Ewenki shaman initiated a new shaman, the senior would make a ritual offering of larches, birches, and willows. When hunters had not been able to hunt down prey for a long time, they would turn to shamans for help, and the shamans would conduct prayers to ask for divine blessings. They would first make a figure of a deer or elk fashioned from willow branches and put it in front of the Malu (hero god noted in Chapter 3), as all the clanspeople looked on. The hunters who asked for the blessings would remove the heads of their bullets to reduce the power and then shoot the willow deer or willow elk. When the bullet went home, all present would simultaneously shout "Well done! well done!" This was quite a serious occasion, and no one was allowed to laugh. After shooting, the hunters pretended to skin the willow deer or willow elk and cut out its entrails, believing that from then on, they could track down wild prey (Inner Mongolia Editorial Committee 1986a:235).

Willow branches and leaves have been regarded as sacred objects also by the Oroqen. When new Oroqen shamans were initiated, they traditionally had to perform a ritual trance dance with senior shamans. They also had to put up a large *sierranju* dwelling centred on two upright willow poles on which they would set two horizontal pine poles and on them a wild duck, the animal commonly used when initiating a new shaman. The willow poles were viewed as a sacred means of access to the heavens. When shamans cured diseases, moreover, they would thank the gods outside the *sierranju*. The *calbalaicin* (presiding shaman) would kneel or stand beside the offerings, holding a willow branch in their right hand. At the end of the chant, the shaman would strip off all its leaves one by one and cast them forwards. The family host would stand at the shaman's side and chant with the shaman.

The Daur traditionally regard the willow as one of their deities. Shamans would hold a Yadagan gathering in the third or fourth lunar month every three years, in which they offered rites to the gods to expel evil spirits and pray for blessings for the whole *mukūn*. Among the deities worshipped in the ritual were twelve Duwalan deities of heaven and earth. Blood was offered to their idols, which were fashioned from tall or thick willows, shrub willows, poplars, or other species of the willow family. Willows have traditionally been used as sacred trees, moreover, in the Daur *yirdeng* shamanic ritual, in which a three-year-old sheep is slain as an offering, and its blood is eaten and a trance dance performed (Inner Mongolia Editorial Committee 1986b:263).

When the Hezhe held their *lushen* rite every March to honour the leaping deer god Tiaolushen (跳鹿神), the rite included a session of skipping the willow. The shaman would bend a willow branch into a semicircle and skip it like a child skipping rope, and all present followed suit: first the shaman family and then the others, each person skipping three times. Moreover, parents would twist a willow branch around their baby's cradle three times while chanting, to symbolize that the child would remain under the deity's protection so as not be struck by misfortune, disease, or evil spirits and be safe and sound their whole life.

The Manchu have likewise regarded willows as endowed with magical power for exorcising illness and evils, and they have many customs expressing their reverence for and worship of willows. Among the Lang, Na, and Guan clans of Huichun, Jilin Province, people performed the ancient fire ritual described in Chapter 3 to show reverence to the sacred willow tree, and they continued to do so up until the foundation of the People's Republic of China in 1949. Even in the 1960s, many Manchu clans continued to perform grand willow rites and the child *huansuo* (换锁) ritual honouring the goddess of fertility Fodo Mama mentioned in Chapter 3. A shaman places a string of colourful threads called *suo* (索, “chain”) around the neck of a young child, believing that the threads will make a girl pretty and healthy and a boy grow up to be a brave *baturu* (hero). Because a willow has numerous leaves and branches, it symbolizes numerous offspring, prosperity, peace, and happiness for the whole clan. In another child’s ritual, a shaman holding an arrow with a long bristle hung on the arrowhead, walks three times around a sacred willow pole pointing up to the heavens, and sprinkles rice wine on the ground. Clan children then scramble to eat *shuituanzi* (水团子), Manchu boiled rice balls, which are stuck on the willow. Both the leafy willow and the *shuituanzi* symbolize numerous progeny. In a ritual to seek childbirth in Heilongjiang, Jilin, and other areas, people would put a willow branch on the tablet of the goddess of fertility Fodo Mama and then fashion grass stalks into the shape of a bird’s nest, which is considered the dwelling place of children’s souls.

In the grand version of the *huansuo* ritual performed by the Jilin Guan clan to worship Fodo Mama, the shaman takes out a *zisunheng* (子孙绳, offspring cord) from a yellow cloth pouch hung under the *weceku* (sacred ancestor niche) above the western *kang* (炕, heatable bed platform) and ties one end of it to the bottom of the *weceku* and the other to a willow branch outside the door. Onto the cord are tied many coloured ribbons which the shaman entwines around the necks of the clan children as *huansuo*. The cords are then brought home, placed on the *weceku* of each child’s home, and then replaced with new ones in the next *jia* ritual.

The *huansuo* ritual was widely inherited and quite common. In still more detail in *News from Heaven* (*Tianzhi ouwen*) a late 19th-century Manchu scholar documents the following:

> The *huansuo* ritual is held from 5 to 7 a.m. A stone is placed below the eastern steps, a willow branch set up on it, and a cord attached. One end of the cord is tied to the right bottom of the sacred niche above the western *kang* and the other end to the branch. New ribbons are hung on the branch in turn with clean papers, a low table with an incense plate is set in front of it, and a clean hemp cord is tied to a sacred arrow at the left of the branch. Women lead their children to kneel down in front of the Willow in turn. After the *huansuo* has been given them, at fish head is sandwiched between a big bun and placed in a crotch of the willow branch. In the afternoon, a servant is ordered to “invite” the willow outside, where he eats the bun and fish head. The willow branch is then hung on the roof, the table and incense taken away, the sacred arrow replaced, and the cord placed in the sacred niche and the ritual is over.
> (Zhen Jun 1982)

Willow worship is related to shaman creation myths. In early Manchu mythology, the goddess of heaven did not have any form. The early image of the heavenly mother goddess Abka Hehe was a giant vulva out of which all things came into being, and the willow was the symbol of the vulva. This gave rise to the myth that a willow gave birth to humans and the world. A shaman text of the Manchu Sitara Hala in Huichun records the following myth:

> Why did the Manchus respect and worship willows? Originally, when Abka Hehe fought against the evil god Yeluli, due to the massive deaths of good gods she had to soar up to heaven. But Yeluli chased after her fast, grabbed her crotch with one hand, and tore off a handful of the willow leaves which were draped over her. The leaves floated down to earth and gave birth to human beings and the world.

Obviously, willow worship in this matriarchal creation myth is closely related to the concept of reverence for women.

In the later patriarchal society, the male deity Abka Enduri became the master of heaven and the universe, but the myths about him were intermingled with the willow worship of the earlier matriarchal society. A sacred text of the Namdulu Hala in Huichun contains the following:

> Long, long ago, when the sky and the earth had just been created, Abka Enduri took off several willow leaves from around his waist, and out of them came flying insects, reptiles, and also humans. From then on, signs of their life-habitation sprung up, and even now, green protuberances housing insects tend to grow on willow leaves like those left by Abka Enduri.

In this myth, the male deity replaces the female, but the matriarchal concept that willows give birth to humans and the world is preserved.

In a myth recorded in a text of the Fuca Hala of Mudanjiang, the initial focus on a male figure shifts in the end to a female generative act:

> In ancient times, the Hurhan Bira (*bira*, "small river" in Manchu) where our Fuca Hala ancestors lived, suddenly turned into the Hurhan Sea, and its glistening white water submerged the world. Of all the males made of the clay rubbed off from Abka Enduri, only one man was left, floating with the tides. Just as he was about to drown, out of nowhere he spied a floating willow branch, seized it and survived. The willow carried him into a stone cave halfway in the water, and there it turned into a beautiful woman, who had intercourse with him and gave birth.

In this myth, willow worship has overtones of clan totem, and the clanspeople of the *hala* traditionally held a ritual to worship willows every year. After the rite, they would reverently place a willow branch in a sacred repository, replace it with a new one when they held the next *jia* ritual, and cast the old one into the river. This enduring yearly rite carried belief in the sacrality of female ancestors into modern times. From it and the other rites just cited, we can trace Manchu beliefs back to the primitive belief of their ancestors that willows were inseparable from the creation goddess as the primordial source of human beings and all creatures in the world. Humans are descendants of willows, and ties of kinship with them are close.

With the passing of time, worship of the willow deity came not to be found not among northern ethnic groups, except for the Manchu. We have concrete records of the willow rituals and games held by their ancestors. Manchu *uleben* (tales) included in *Record of the Grievances of the East Sea* speak of the Donghai Weji tribe offering willows to the water deity and the sea, and the most famous willow rite of all is that of the Russian Donghai Gahutanhe tribe associated with the seat of the Weji khan. The rite was held when the sea tide went out, rivers dried up, a plague broke out, or green protuberances appeared on willow leaves. The khanum Sihulin would then select nine, seventeen, or as many as thirty-three beautiful women to represent the willow and sea deities, naked except for willow girdles around their waists. The tribespeople would group around the women, sprinkling deer blood, rice wine, and clear river water on their bodies as they shouted and echoed the dancing women's song. As a female shaman began to shake her waist bells and beat her sacred drum, the women would follow her to all areas of the tribe – mountains, wilds, and riverbanks – lively walking, dancing, singing, and shouting along the way. Wherever they trod was sprinkled with deer blood and river water to worship the willow deity, sea deity, and other deities so that they would bless the tribe with peace and a good harvest. During the ceremony, the women were not allowed to go home but rather had to live on the water. Nowadays, this kind of ritual no longer exists, but while doing fieldwork in Huichun, I heard Manchus speak of how similar activities were held during the Manchukuo period of the 1930s and 1940s, but with the women representing the willow deity dressed in their clothes.

The sacrality of willows is also highlighted in in their use as idols. The Manchu have traditionally carved spirit idols out of willow, known as willow men or willow deities. They also fashioned various bird and other animal deities out of willow, and they made sacred ritual implements out of thick willow wood: *gida* (gun) barrels, arrow shafts, and sacred poles on which to hang *wadan* (pouches). The Donhai Jurchen epic *Umesiben Mama* records the use of willow wood by the Weji tribe in rites to worship fish. Before the ritual, fish-shaped sacrificial cakes were made of glutinous millet threshed in golden winds, and a fish-shaped spirit idol the size of two or three people was made of new, thick willow branches along the river. Apart from the fins, which were made of white swan feathers, the idol was made of fresh, tender willow branches and leaves, and it was shaped into various lifelike animated poses – jumping, flying, swimming, or one fish biting the tail of another. During the rite, youths good at swimming were chosen to worm their way into the fish-shaped spirit idols, and each would briefly touch the fish gills, sway the fish tails, and dive into the water and rise to the surface like a school of fish playing. The kanum wore willow beading, the presiding female shaman and participating clanspeople wrapped willow leaves around their bodies, and both children and adults wore fish-shaped hats made of willow branches or bark. The hats had various shapes – carp head, whale head, and flying fish head. The river and its banks were alive everywhere with these fish-shaped idols, fish dances, and fish songs, as if the whole ritual were held in the submarine Dragon Palace replete with many kinds of fish – truly a world of fish and willows. The rite lasted three days and three nights, during which time all the clanspeople, old and young alike, lived on the riverside or on *weihū* (boats) on the water. They consumed willow leaves, fish, shrimp, deer blood, and river water. Only in this way could the fish god Medehe Enduri grant them abundant fish.

As an offshoot of willow rituals, willows games were an amusing source of entertainment among Manchu ancestors. In the late Ming and early Qing periods, one such game was *paoliucheng* (跑柳城, running the Willow Walls). As depicted in *Legend of Nurhaci and Wanggao* (*Liangshi hanwangzhuan*), girls selected as the tiger head queen or willow queen would wear a tiger-pelt blouse, willow skirt, and willow garland, and two teams would try to capture the queen of the other side and keep her in the submarine Dragon Palace. When a team's queen was captured, it would choose a second and then third queen and so on, and the team that had no tiger head queen left lost. It was said that when the Jianzhou Jurchen (建州) leader Wanggao went to the Ula tribe to visit Dolo Khan, he saw many young women happily playing this game.

5.4 Bear rituals

The peoples of northern China have long held such animals as bears, tigers, wolves, and snakes in awe and dealt with them reverently. They have many rituals and myths, moreover, revering the bear god. As we noted in Chapter 2, Siberian peoples such as the Nivkh, Ewenki, Hezhe, and Udege have also long worshipped the bear. The Nivkh (formerly Gilyak) traditionally celebrated a bear festival and had bear sacrifice. The Ewenki and Oroqen in China also venerate bears. The Oroqen language word for bear is *nionioku*, but people never refer to them as such; they call them *amaha* (uncle) and more specifically male bears *yaya* (grandfather) and female bears *taitie* (grandmother). When they capture a bear, they carry it home but pretend to weep for it, and when they eat its meat, they conduct a wind burial for the bones, hanging them on a tree. They also hold a rite for skinning a bear and distribute the bear hide with great respect. The Ewenki actually believed that bears were formerly human beings but that because they committed mistakes, they were condemned to become beasts and walk on four legs. The Ewenki think that they, themselves, are actually human bears and hold wind burials for these "uncles" in a way that is quite similar to the Oroqen. The Ewenki believe that if they just toss out their bones without a proper wind burial, the bears will be unable to return to their caves to hibernate and hunters will thus not be able to easily capture them and, what's worse, will run the risk of being mauled by them.

The Ewenki wind burial commonly follows several set steps. First, hunters capture a bear, skin it, and wrap its body parts with birch bark entwined sixfold with willow branches. They do so with its head, throat, tongue, nose, neck bone, small leg bones, paw bones, two upper-right ribs, two lower-right ribs, and two upper-left ribs. To prepare the burial site, they then strip the bark off of two pines from a southern slope exposed to the sun, carve twelve horizontal grooves on the flat surfaces of the stripped tree, and colour the grooves with various tints, using charcoal, blood, and the juices of wild flowers. Next, they inlay the bear's eyes in the two ends of the sixth groove and hang the bones and wrapped body parts between the two pines to complete the wind burial. People pretend once more to weep for the bear. They preserve the bearskin but toss out the rest. The Ewenki do not perform a wind burial for bears that have mauled people, but in general, they have traditionally viewed bears in a special way and disposed of them in a reverential manner.

The Daur have also held bears in veneration. Among their *wenggure* (deities) worshipped in *ye* rituals, tigers and bears occupy an important place, and in the Daur folktale "The Hero Shi'en and Maiden Zhang Lihua," an elderly man and woman who help the maiden are an *atirekan* (male bear) and *etire* (female bear).

Manchu bear rituals have a unique form. As is stated in *Tangyuan Annals* (*Tangyuan xianzhi*),

> In the past, the banks of the Sungari (Songhua) River was the dwelling place of the Feiyaka (Gilyak) tribe, who liked to tease bears as *mafa* (grandpa). People regularly bought bears at a high price, domesticated them, and then let relatives, friends, and neighbors shoot them for entertainment. There were two kinds of bears that people used for this purpose in northern China: the Tibetan blue bear and the Asian black bear. People killed them and then gathered to eat the meat. First, they ate the head in the wilds to show respect to the elders; they then ate the remaining parts of the bear at home, women eating only the legs. A third species of bear – brown bear – also often appeared in the mountains. When hunters captured them, they made use only of their gallbladder.
>
> (Tangyuan Annals Editorial Committee 1992)

The same document gives details of Feiyaka tribespeople's playfully teasing bears, from which we can see that they treated them with a certain degree of respect.

The Manchu praise bears for their boldness and loyalty and regard them as guardians of light for human beings. The bear god is a giant deity with invincible strength, and when shamans are possessed by him, they can lift a millstone, uproot a huge willow, or toss chunk balls of stone, displaying the humanlike boldness, bravery, and invincibility of bears. In the Manchu fire ritual, the infinitely powerful bear god is the trailblazer of the sun god, and in the Manchu myth "War in Heaven," the bear is called Lefu Mafa (*Lefu* meaning "bear" and *Mafa* "grandfather") and is the first being to have a human *coco* (male genitals). When Lefu Mafa fought against the evil god Yeluli, however, he shirked his duty and fell asleep among grape vines by the Amur River, resulting in Yeluli being able to knock many stars out of the Milky Way, which would become meteors.

Of the numerous sacred Manchu lyrics that I collected, the bear ritual is documented in all *ye* ritual texts. From this, we can conclude that the worship of the bear god is ancient and widespread. The rules of the shamanic rituals of the Xu, Zang, and He clans specify that bear hide must not be used to make drumheads or idols. The Manchu believe that if a drumhead is made of bear hide, it will crack, and if a shaman performs a trance dance to summon the bear god, the god will cause pandemonium and bring calamity upon the shaman and the ritual host. Therefore, to ensure that things go smoothly, only the hides of deer, elk, and cattle are traditionally made into drumheads. Today's northern peoples have now long engaged in farming, not hunting, but various Manchu clans still respect bears and fear them as humanlike animals who can potentially seek revenge. This mentality is believed to be a remnant of ancient bear totemism, which I find reasonable. In general, moreover, it shows that the formation and development of northern peoples' cultural mindset has a coherent, common foundation.

Bears are not the only animal revered in the North; other fierce wild animals such as tigers and wolves have also been held as sacred beasts, the tiger god being worshipped among the Oroqen, Ewenki, Hezhe, and Daur. The Oroqen name for the tiger god is Borukan, but he is also called Bainaca (mountain god), the mountain god being the tiger god who later became an elder with white hair. In general, the Oroqen call tigers *niocita* (great-grandfather), and they call wolves not *gusige* (wolf) but *weng*, after the sound of their call. Northern peoples also venerate leopards, jackals, and other beasts of the wilds; whales, sharks, snakeheads, pikes, turtles, and other aquatic animals; and hedgehogs and other small animals. In some clans, people enshrine the skins and bones of these animals as spirit idols, which they use as substitutes for the animals in sacrificial rituals. In *ye* rituals in the past, various ethnic peoples summoned these animal deities, and once they descended upon the altar, shamans and their assistants would mimic their natural traits in entertaining stunts. After they played for a while in this way, they would then reverently send them back to their divine world.

5.5 Snake worship

Besides powerful mammals, some cold-blooded animals have also held a special position in shaman worship, especially serpents. They are respected and protected by the python god, also called the snake god, which is worshipped in shaman rites of the Manchu, Hezhe, Daur, Xibe, Oroqen, Ewenki, and other northern peoples. In Manchu rites, the python is distinguished from other snakes by its size, pythons measuring nine *chi*尺and snakes eight *chi* (1 *chi* equals about 33.3 cm). For the Manchu, Daur, and other ethnic groups, the snake deity idol is binary, male and female always together, as in the following Daur spirit idol of the snake god carved out of wood:

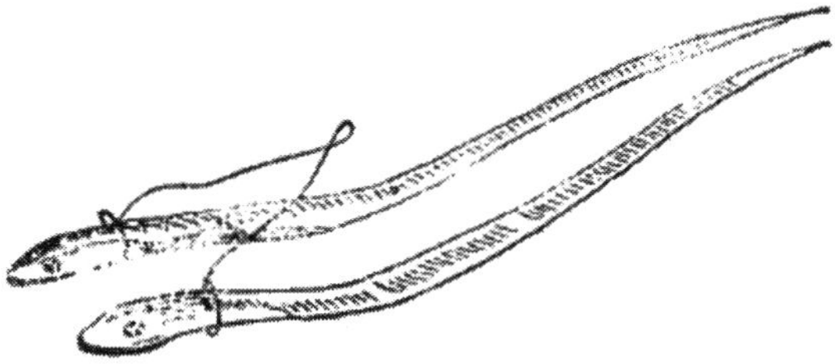

Snake patterns are commonly found on shamanic ritual garb. In the *ye* rites of many Manchu clans, a python skin is sewn on the shaman's costume, and several snake-bone pendants are hung on the ritual headdress to allow the shaman to be able to see light in darkness. The sacred skirt of the great shamaness Umesiben in the Manchu epic *Umesiben Mama* was made of the inner skins of ninety-nine serpents of five colours.

The most difficult ritual gesture to be learned by shaman candidates in Manchu *Jiao'uyun* training sessions is mimicking a snake's slithering crawl. They must lay on their backs and use the strength of their shoulders to swiftly move forwards in criss-cross fashion. All Manchu shamans can imitate a serpent's crawl, and the more swiftly one can do so, the more powerful the shaman. When the python god possesses a shaman of the Xu clan of Suihua, Heilongjiang, the shaman not only crawls on their back but can also worm their way up a wall or straw curtain without dropping to the ground, quite like a martial art *qinggong*[2] feat.

For the Gilyak and many other peoples north of the Amur, serpent deities symbolize spring, the sun, light and warmth, and the Ainu on the Japanese Archipelago venerate the snake as the sun god. In Ainu mythology, the snake never descends upon the earth alone but always comes with his goddess lover, the sun. In some sacred Manchu texts, the snake is called the light of the sun, or serpent light: "a beam of light that descends to the earth like a snake."[3] It is reasonable that people understood snakes as a symbol of the sun and light. Because northern serpents prefer a humid habitat, their scales can eventually fester and maggots can breed if they do not sun themselves on sunny days. So when sunrays reappear after a rainfall, snakes wriggle out of their caves and coil themselves on rocks and logs, exposing themselves to the sun. On the basis of long-term observation of these creatures, primitive humans could well have believed that the snake was the messenger of the sun and so revered them as a sun deity.

Lizards have also traditionally been worshipped in the North. They are worshipped as a small deity in the dark that can foretell weather and flooding and indicate directions. As the assistant and messenger of the serpent deity, they also predict the arrival of the sun and sunlight. A lizard can heal snake wounds, and its saliva is treasured for its agglutinate effect on broken bones and the healing of open wounds. When shamans treat wounds, they often smash a lizard to death and apply its viscera to the wound. When they simultaneously invoke the lizard god and snake god, the wound heals quickly. Lizard patterns are painted on the shamanic garb of several ethnic peoples, and lizards are used as charms. In 1982, I saw several small dried black lizards that had been preserved intact for more than twenty years by shaman Yan Zhenkuan (阎振宽) in his home in Yongji, Jilin Province. When asked why he had preserved them for so long and what they were used for, he said they were talismans that had been passed down by shamans for generations and that they could exorcise evil spirits and ward off the effects of snake venom. Among the various deities that Yan Zhenkuan worshipped, there were two white serpent gods from the mountains of the upper reaches of the Sungari River. If people invoked them by offering nine small lizards, they would descend. He said it was amazing that people could know the time and direction of the gods' arrival from a lizard's twitching. He gave these details with great solemnity, stressing that snake rituals are just as important as the bear ritual. Another shaman, Yang Shichang (杨世昌), once said that he could summon two python gods who dwelt near the East Sea. When he was possessed by one of them, he felt chilly and then lost his senses. He said, too, that normally he would not capture snakes, nor could he even easily see snakes, though other people could readily capture or restrain snakes in the wild by stepping on them. He also worshipped the lizard, believing it to be shamans' mentor. He hadn't seen a lizard for seventy years but heard this from his own mentor.

Why have northern peoples worshipped the snake god? Shirokogoroff once suggested that snake worship proves that northern Tungus shamanism originated in the South. In fact, however, Snake totems have long existed among the ethnic peoples of northeast China and Siberia, and the snake was absorbed into their shamanic systems. Many scholars long believed that in the North there are indeed snakes, but no pythons, so they surmised that python rituals may have originated with the Han Chinese or at least that this northern tradition had been influenced by southern Chinese culture. However, I heard the elders say that huge pythons were once in northeast China. Several eighty-year-old elders in Huichun claimed separately that they had seen a huge python sinking its head in the river to quench its thirst, with its body on a cliff or in a cave of the mountains near the village of Madida. Their accounts indicate that that serpent was quite long. Similar accounts have been heard from elders in Dongning in Jilin Province and Tonghua in Heilongjiang. *Collected Records of Changbai Mountain* (*Changbai zhengcunlu* 1910) documents that "the local snakes are mostly black and that serpents as long as several *zhang* (丈, 1 *zhang* being 3.58 metres) could be found in the forests and some over one *chi* in girth in the undergrowth and hills" (Zhang Fengtai and Liu Longguang 1910). *Huinan Annals* (*Huinan xianzhi*) records that serpents of various kinds are often seen in the mountains, the bigger ones several *zhang* long and as thick as a *yu* (broad-mouthed liquid container) (Bai Chunyi and Yu Fengtong 1927). These records substantiate that there were pythons in the northeastern mountains in times gone past that posed a great threat to the populace, especially to those who lived in the forests.

In more traditional accounts, in the mythical legends of *Classic of Mountains and Seas* (*Shanhai jing*) from the 3rd century BCE to the 2nd century CE, there was a mountain in the great northern wilderness named Buxian Shan where there was a country called Sushen, where their existed insects with four wings and animals with a beast's head and a snake's body called *qinchong* (琴虫) (Liu Xin 1989). That legendary Chinese animal may have been a reptile or giant lizard. In any case, people were frequently attacked by fierce reptiles and out of human weakness and fear turned to worshipping them in the hope that these powerful beings would show them mercy and protect them, not harm them. The Manchu *Record of the Grievances of the East Sea* depicts pythons coiling around human bodies and strangling them to death in just a few minutes with a tight grip that would break their bones. In addition to casualties caused by large pythons, mountain cave dwellers were frequently attacked by smaller serpents. Snake worship was a cultural response to people's fright and awe (Fu Yuguang 2007).

Another impetus for worshipping the snake and its description in the art and mythology of ancient northern Asian peoples is that they desired the presence of serpents. Snakes are ubiquitous and can hide in any tiny space. No intricate cave, tree hole, cranny, or crack in a rock formation can elude their eyes. When primitive human beings sought to plumb the mysteries of life, they thus believed that the snake could assist them. As mediators between deities and humans, clan shamans hoped to possess the snake's divine inspiration and mystical power. This partly explains why serpent images appear in every decorative item of a shaman's ritual garb.

People have worshipped serpents, too, for their procreative power, believing that they can bring them an abundance of offspring. The Manchu shaman Yang Shichang mentioned earlier once said that worshipping the snake god and praying for child blessing can heal menstruation-related diseases. Some people, moreover, that snakes are licentious and can copulate not only with their own species but also with turtles. Thus, folklore tales speak of a hybrid turtle snake. The Manchu *Legends of Nurhaci and Wanggao* (*Liangshi hanwangzhuan*), recounts that Wanggao, the tribal hero of the Jianzhou Jurchen, was born near a pool in response to his mother's morning prayers when a celestial snake copulated with a sacred turtle in dense fog. His mother breathed in the spermous air, became impregnated, and thus gave birth. Like some other Chinese and foreign myths, this myth reflects the idea that serpents have a kind of blood relationship with human beings. In ancient Chinese myths, Nüwa (女娲), the mother goddess known for creating humankind and repairing the pillar of heaven, is portrayed with a human head and snake's body. Some also believe that snakes can copulate continually and that the snake god can heal impotence and sterility. People thus worship the snake also because of this curative power.

For examples of snake worship outside China, look to the Dravidians in South India, where a childless couple sometimes offers sacrifice to an image of two snakes coiled together as a symbol of copulation. On the Fiji Islands, snakes are regarded as the incarnation of a revered deity. The Ainus in Japan never kill snakes or eat snake meat; instead, they hang or place snake icons on their most important and sacred places, such as by a lampstand, the hearth, or the enshrined tablets of family ancestors.

Finally, snakes are the most powerful protective deities of the shamans of northern China, and shamans patronized by the snake god are, themselves, considered the most powerful. When a snake possesses a shaman, that shaman can perform miraculous feats.

Notes

1 The elders are Fu Jixiang 付吉祥, Gao Qishan 高岐山, Yan Wenkuan 阎文宽, and Guan Zhiyuan 关志远.

2 *Qinggong*轻功 is a legendary technique in which a martial artist is alleged to have the ability to move swiftly and lightly at superhuman speed and perform gravity-defying moves such as gliding on water surfaces, scaling high walls, and mounting trees.

3 See *Translation of the Sacred Texts of Manchu Xu Clan* (Sumu Hala), unpublished.

6 Tangse and jia rituals

Since the Manchu Qing dynasty, there have been basically two kinds of shamanic rituals in northern China: the Qing imperial *tangse* rituals performed at the state Tangse Shrine in the southeast of the Forbidden City and the *jia* folk rituals of commoners. The Qing *tangse* rituals were an evolved but in some way corrupted form of the shamanic folk rituals of the Manchu and other northern peoples. The *jia* rituals were the standardized form of shamanic folk rites as influenced by the Qing court rituals. The two have similarities as well as differences. On the most basic level, the Qing *tangse* rituals drew upon Manchu folk traditions but were fettered by the set procedures of the palace worship of preceding dynasties. Although unfettered by ritual regulations and disciplinary rubrics, the jia folk rites have varied contents, forms, and sacrificial procedures which are also quite complicated.

6.1 Tangse rituals

A summary account of the Qing rites held at the imperial Tangse Shrine is given in *Encyclopedia of Imperial Documents: Rites Honoring the Heaven and the Earth* (*Huangchao wenxian tongkao jiaoshekao*), the 1787 Qing work covering the period from the beginning of the dynasty in 1616 to 1785:

> At the beginning of his reign, Nurhaci of the Qing dynasty established the tradition of worship in a visitation to a temple. Rites were held for important state events, on New Year's Day and on the first day of every lunar month at the Tangse Shrine. Before an important journey or excursion, prayers are first offered at the Tangse, and before a military campaign and after a triumphal return, prayers are also offered at the Tangse, which is all ceremoniously lined with military banners.

A more detailed account is given in the early-19th-century work *Miscellaneous Records of Xiaoting* (*Xiaoting zalu*):

> The Qing dynasty had the tradition of worshipping heaven in a manner that originated in Shenyang, Liaoning Province, in which sacred standards were

> erected. In a peaceful hall known as Tangse gods of the soil and grain were also worshipped, in accord with old Ming traditions. When the Qing Empire established its capital in Beijing, a Tangse was built outside the Chang'an Left Gate. A shrine where all deities could be worshipped was constructed at the center of the Tangse court facing south. In front and to the south of it, a circular shrine for worshipping heaven was constructed, and in the middle of the court, there was a stone pedestal with a hole for erecting the emperor's sacred standard. On the right and left behind the standard were lined six rows of six stone pedestals, each with sacred holes where other ritual standards would be erected, the first row for the sons of the emperor and the second, third, fourth, fifth and sixth rows in turn for princes of the first rank (*qinwang*,亲王), princes of the second rank (*junwang*,郡王), princes of the third rank (*beile*贝勒, meaning "lord," "prince" or "chief" in Manchu), princes of the fourth rank (*beizi*, 贝子), and various dukes and counts.
>
> (Zhao Hui 1980)

A still-more-detailed account is given in *History of the Qing*: *Treatise 60, Rite 4* (*Qingshigao zhiliushi lisi*) of the 1929 encyclopaedic work praising the Qing dynasty by elderly Qing survivors:

> The custom of worshipping heaven in the Tangse Shrine had its origins at the beginning of the Qing dynasty in Shenyang, Liaoning Province. In the Beijing Tangse, sacred standard poles were erected to send tribute to heaven. The shrine was a peaceful edifice in which various deities were worshipped. When Qing Emperor Shunzhi (顺治, 1638–1661) established the capital at Yanjing (燕京, present-day Beijing), the Tangse was ordered to be built according to tradition outside the Chang'an Left Gate. In the middle, there were five shrines facing south with glazed tile roofs, in which various deities were enshrined. In front of them, the shrine for worshipping heaven was constructed facing north. To the south and in the middle of this shrine was the emperor's stone pedestal with a hole for his sacred standard. On each side of the emperor's standard, there were six rows of six stone pedestals with holes for sacred standards. The first row was for the sons of the emperor and then the second, third, fourth, fifth and sixth rows in turn for princes of the first, second, third, and fourth ranks and various dukes. At the southeast of the Tangse, there were three shrines facing south, known as the sacred deity shrines. For worshipping heaven on New Year's Day, praying before a military campaign, or celebrating a triumphal return, the emperor would perform the sacrificial rite at these shrines in person. For the monthly rituals, as well as for sacred pole rituals, horse rituals, and the Buddha's birthday celebration on the eighth day of the fourth month of the Chinese lunar calendar, the emperor would send representatives to perform the rites. Emperor Chongde (崇德) made it a rule in the first year of his reign (1626) that on New Year's Day, the emperor, princes of the first rank, and the vice dutong (副都统, banner head) should perform the sacrifice.

According to another section of the 1929 encyclopaedic work, volume 92 of *Qing Dynasty Decrees and Regulations* (*Qinghuidian*), among the various Manchu rites worshipping heaven and other gods, some were held during the day, others at night. The deities worshipped during the day were Śākyamuni Buddha, Avalokiteśvara, and deified 2nd-century Chinese General Guan Di (Guan Yu, 关羽), which are not Indigenous shamanist deities but "guest gods" that shamanism had come to worship under the influence of Buddhism and the religious beliefs of the Han Chinese. Several other deities were worshipped at night.[1]

Among Qing imperial rites, the *zhao* (朝祭, dawn) rite was held from 3:00 a.m. to 5:00 a.m. and the *xi* (夕祭, dusk) rite from 3:00 p.m. to 5:00 p.m. Both were held in the emperor's Qingning Palace (清宁宫) and, after the capital was moved to Beijing, in Kunning Palace (坤宁宫). The *zhao* rite was held on the west *kang* of the palace and the *xi* rite on the north *kang* in the west chamber. The deities worshipped in the Qing *tangse* rites were ancestor gods of the imperial Manchu Aisin Gioro clan, along with nature and animal deities worshipped for generations as the protective gods of the clan. The rigid imperial rituals promoted during the reign of Emperor Qianlong in the 18th century are well documented in *Manchu Trance Rites for the Worship of Heaven* (*Manzhou tiaoshen jitian dianli*), but the details of these rites are too extensive and repetitive to give here.

"*Tangse*" came to be the official term used for the edifice used for imperial rituals in the *Veritable Records of the Founding Emperor Nurhaci* (*Taigzugao huangdi shilu*), composed in 1749, the fourteenth year of the reign of Qianlong (乾隆). Previously, the word "*miao*" (庙, shrine, temple) had been commonly used for that edifice. The term "*tangse*" cannot be interpreted literally as an edifice, but it is appropriate because the content and character of the court *tangse* rituals resembled the Indigenous northern shaman *ye* rites worshipping deities enshrined in the traditional Manchu *tangse*. Ye rituals summoning a deity who would possess an entranced shaman were popular among nomadic tribes before the Liao and subsequent Jin dynasties (907–1234). For the ancient Jurchen, such rites included the worship of heaven, fire, water, sea, stars, and trees, and they were held even as people migrated. They would then take their deities with them in sacred coffers, also called *tangse*, and later, when they ceased their nomadic ways, they revered them in actual buildings, called *tangse*.

I discovered from documents unearthed in records of the Nurhaci clan, the *Legends of Nurhaci and Wanggao (Liangshi hanwang zhuan)*, and the *Legend of General Sabusu* (*Sadaren zhuan*) that has circulated in the Aihui area of Heilongjiang for almost three centuries that *tangse* folk rituals have long been practised by the northern peoples of China. Historian Meng Sen (孟森), citing *Records of Yongxian* (*Yongxian lu*) concerning early-18th-century Qing history, wrote that northern trance-dance rituals originated from the Huihe township of Aihui and that *tangse* rituals did not originate with the Manchu (Xiao Shi 1997). However, Manchu genealogies and shaman texts demonstrate that "*tangse*" is a Manchu term commonly used early in the Jurchen era, derived from the Manchu word *dangse*, meaning "archive."

The heads of the various Manchu clans preserved an Enduri pack of enshrined deities and a *tangse* pack of tribal genealogies, spirit tablets, sacred texts and instruments, and portraits of ancestors and deities. These packs enshrined deities, but they were not buildings. They were the tablets of the deities that nomadic clans carried with them and would enshrine in their yurts when they set them up. They put spirit idols, portraits of the ancestors, and sacred texts and instruments mostly in birch, willow, and other wooden or bone cases or in stone or earthen pots, which they then placed in rectangular chests with moveable lids as "sacred coffers," known as *tangse*. The deities thus lived with humans in the same dwelling. This was a long tradition among Manchu and other northern peoples.

Later, when people settled down, they constructed *tangse* buildings, the form of which became gradually fixed, and passed them down to new generations in accordance with Manchu modes of life and religious beliefs. Before Nurhaci, chief of the Jianzhou Jurchens, unified other Jurchen tribes at the beginning of the 17th century, clan *tangse* were regularly established in the hoton (town) where the tribal chieftain (*khan* or *da* in Manchu) lived. At that time, the word "*tangse*" was also written *tangshe* or *dangse*, all transliterations of *tangse*: a holy place for worshipping guardian spirits and ancestral gods. The size and construction materials varied among tribes. In some large tribes, there were both the main *tangse* and branch *tangse* for *mukūn* subtribes, all similar to the Qing court *tangse* built later by the Aisin Gioro clan.

Concerning the *tangse* edifice of the Hada tribe of the 16th-century alliance of Seven Jurchen Hulun tribes mentioned in Chapter 3 that Nurhaci eventually conquered, *Legends of Nurhaci and Wanggao* records that with the help of the Ming government, the Hada Khan Wan once aspired to the paramount leadership of all the tribes. When his mother, Dong Eji, celebrated her eightieth birthday, the chieftains of four tribes in the Hulun Alliance, along with leaders of the Jianzhou Left Guard and Right Guard, assembled their forces and offered prayers for her at the Xiachang Tangse, the magnificent Hada *tangse* edifice. In another incident, when the leader of the Jianzhou Right Guard, Wang Gao (王杲), borrowed troops from the Donghai Weji tribe, that tribe's chieftain brought Wang to worship at his *tangse* and later married off his daughter to Wang. When Nurhaci later conquered the Hada, Hūfa, Yehe, and Ula tribes, he regularly destroyed their *tangse* and plundered their ancestral portraits and genealogies. As an aid in the unification of Jurchen tribes, he established the Manchu Eight Banners (八旗) that would form part of the military and political system of the Qing dynasty.[2] Early in the reign of Qing Emperor Huang Taiji (皇太极) in the 17th century, the emperor ordered the Manchu administrative banners to stop building *tangse*. As we have just seen, however, Manchu clans had long been housing their portable *tangse* in their yurts. As a more evolved form of ancestor worship, the *tangse* in the Qing court came to include all the universal deities recognized by the Jurchen ancestors of the Manchu. Apart from the ancient ancestral gods of the Aisin Gioro clan were also *nohontaiji* (god of heaven) and *uduben beise* (primordial ancestors), which frequently appear in the records of Manchu clans and were worshipped in routine rituals as both universal deities and tribal ancestral gods. In a Manchu dialect, "*nohon*" refers to the colour pea green or bluish green. So in some sacred texts, *nohon abka* means "blue sky" or "heaven," and shamans interpret *nohon taiji* (*nohon anji* in shaman texts of *dongjing, heilongiang*) as "the god of heaven," which I regard as correct. *Uduben beise* (also recorded as *wuzhu beizi, wudu beise*, etc.) refers to primordial ancestors. Many believed that various nature deities, ancient ancestors, and hero gods of one's own tribe lived in the heavens after death, and their idols or icons were preserved. The seedling god was also worshipped, demonstrating that praying for a good harvest was common among the rituals honouring the gods of heaven and pointing to a boom in agrarian economy in feudal societies.

The rituals in the Beijing Kunning Palace mentioned earlier were similar to those held by the common public but simplified. The shamanic *zhao* (dawn) rituals there included, however, the worship of non-Indigenous deities, such as Bodhisattva, and Guan Di. The evening *xi* rituals worshipped clan ancestor gods and the deities that had been worshipped by Jurchen tribes for generations, such as the star gods Enduri Sengge and Nadan Daihūn invoked for protecting the family household and bringing peace.

In ordinary folk rites, most Manchu clans did not worship the foregoing three Han deities but stuck strictly to their own shamanist traditions. There is no doubt that some clans worshipped Bodhisattva Avalokiteśvara in the *jia* rituals (*jiaji* 家祭) influenced by the court rituals, but such foreign deities were not honoured with ritual offerings or individual eulogies. The statue of Avalokiteśvara was simply placed beside the sacred curtain for worship along with other deities.

By comparing the ancestral deities worshipped in the court *xi* rituals and those worshipped among Manchu clan commoners, one finds that many gods with the same or similar names were included in both. Such, for example, are Ahun Niyansi and other deities found in the more than forty hand-copied clan texts that I collected. Although the Chinese transcriptions of the names sometimes differ, it is not difficult to identify them as referring to the same god, indicating that the deities worshipped in the *xi* rituals were not only the ancestor gods of the imperial Aisin Gioro clan but also those worshipped by Jurchen tribes in earlier days. Another case in point is the various names of the Jurchen ancestral protective deity of the wood or boar skin spirit idol Muli Khan (Chinese transcription Mao'er Khan), who is also called Mulin Kahn, Biganyi Mafa, and Biganyi Enduri. I think that Muli is a Tungus word referring to the deity Borukan worshipped by many northern peoples. Still another example is Katun Noyan, which is referred to in various documents also as Gatun Nuoyin, Katun Panyan, and Katun Nayan. This deity is regarded as a Mongol god in some historical accounts; as is commonly known, however, Manchu clans did not worship deities of other clans or tribes, and the same was true for Kunning Palace rituals. This god is a Manchu deity, not a Mongol deity. Despite the various pronunciations of the name, Gatun Nuoyin can be recognized as the same protective deity worshipped by the Jurchen and Manchu ancestors living in the Changbai Mountain and along the Sungari and Mudan rivers. In fact, the divine power of Katun Noyan was omnipresent in northeast China. The worship of "portrait gods" was little known in the court *tangse xi* rites, but

Manchu clans had the tradition of making coloured ancestor portraits that were respectfully preserved in a sacred coffer on the *weceku* ancestor niche on the west wall of the main room. The portraits were hung, repaired, and worshipped during the Spring Festival, in spring and autumn rituals, and in the years of the dragon, tiger, rat, and snake according to the stems and branches (*gangzhi*, 干支) calendrical cycle of sixty signs marking days or years. In the past, people used straw, wood, stone, leather, silk, and other materials to make these spirit portrait idols; with modern painting skills, people now use coloured drawings and photocopies. Oroqen, Ewenki, Daur, Mongol, and Xibe clans neighbouring the Manchu have also had this tradition. Most of the portraits are those of *da mafa* (primogenitor or remote ancestor). In portraits of the Manchu Li Hala in Ning'an, Heilongjiang, the top of the picture depicts the moon on the left, stars on the right, the Big Dipper in the sky, and a sacred bird perched on the ancestral soul tree. The ancestor is drawn on the lower part of the canvas, with a chart stating his major exploits and a list of his fine steeds and domestic animals. People worshipped only the ancestor portraits of their own clans, not those of other clans. The 13th-century *Khitan Chronicles* (*Qidan guozhi*) records that "the deities worshipped should not be disturbed by those of other clans" (Ye Longli 1985).

Some court *tangze* rituals followed the common Manchu folk tradition of holding a memorial to worship deities whom they believed have special powers to cure an epidemic or contagious disease. For instance, Ming General Deng Zuo (邓佐) was one of the smallpox gods worshipped in *tangse* rituals. Like other northern ethnic groups, primitive Jurchens and Manchus were fearful of the various pestilences and plagues that could affect the clan's populace. Smallpox could wipe out an entire clan and in ancient Manchu shaman texts is called *shantaha* (white devil). Manchu shamans devoutly believed in goddesses who could dispel the bane of smallpox and called them mama goddess, among whom are Talaha Mama and Fodo Mama. In the folk custom of *zoubaibing* (走百病), "walking a hundred diseases," on the fifteenth or sixteenth day of the first lunar month, people would take a stroll in groups and cross every bridge they met, in the hope that this would keep them free from baneful spirits. Other customs handed down from the Jurchen period to eradicate smallpox, ward off threats of disaster, and pursue happiness are *sheliutiaohuo* (射柳跳火), shooting at willows and running over burning coals, and *dahuami* (打画迷), blackening one's hands with soot from a pan bottom and then smearing it on women's faces in imitation of the legendary Aunt Zhaoli.

The court *tangse* rituals preserved some of the original features of the rituals of the Aisin Gioro Hala of the Qing rulers. As we have said, however, they were both influenced and hemmed in by the set practices of palace worship of preceding dynasties. Therefore, they gradually became standardized palace-like, temple-like affairs, and their Indigenous ethnic traits suffered considerable loss. In particular, with the alterations and "enrichments" carried out during the reigns of the Qianlong Daoguang emperors (1711–1850), the vividness, literary vitality and strong northern cultural features of the traditional shaman chants became empty, stylized eulogies droned out in extremely rigid rites. As a merger of sacrificial rites from past dynasties, they constitute a rare cultural heritage for scholars to retrace the evolution of court rituals, but they suffered a great loss in content and value for people's daily life.

6.2 Manchu jia rituals

Concerning the Manchu *jia* rituals held by the standard-bearers (*qiren* 旗人, militarily and politically organized Qing commoners), the 1934 encyclopaedic *Records of Mukden* (*Fengtian tongzhi*) quotes from the 1777 Qing dynasty work *Researches on Manchu Origins* (*Manzhou yuanliu kao*) as follows:

> Ever since the beginning of our dynasty, we have constructed *tangse*, erected sacred poles to worship heaven with great respect, and placed deity tablets in the main hall of the imperial worship chamber. From this we know that the Manchu custom of worshipping sacred poles and deity tablets has had a long history. The bannermen inherited this custom, with instruments and procedures varying according to the following rules. The west wall of the family room or west chamber of the house is regarded as a sacred area because it is reserved for the deity tablets. They are usually kept on a board hung with yellow satin curtains or stored in a wooden chest covered with colored silk strips several *chi* (尺 = 1/3 meter) long. Sometimes the chest is placed on the sacred board with four or five coils of incense and is treated the same as spirit tablets. The tablets of Wanli Mama or Fodo Mama are set to the left of the chest. This goddess does not have a portrait; instead, there is a silk pouch attached to the tablet, in which there are cords of five colors, six or seven *zhang* (丈 = 3 1/3 meters) in length and known as *suo* (锁, chain lock). Under the southwest roof, a long wooden board enshrines portraits of Guan Di and Avalokiteśvara painted on silk, beneath which is a narrow *kang* on which nobody is allowed to sit or sleep.

People set up an altar table there and twisted straw into ropes to bind up the sacrificial animal. In the south corner of the courtyard, they erected the *somoimoo* (sacred pole) and put a tin plate on the top.

The account of the *jia* ritual in the 1777 Qing work continues as followed:

> Families of the bannermen usually conducted a sacrificial rite lasting three days twice a year, in spring and autumn. Before the rite, they should fast, and during the course of the rite, they get up early and clean the west *kang*. They hang up the silk painting of Guan Di and set before it a table with three cups of liquor. They also set up a rectangular wooden brazier and cast into it purple Asian rhododendron petals used for incense, and they make flat steamed broomcorn millet cakes sprinkled with sesame as sacrificial offerings. After they get up on the first day of the rite, the family worship Guan Di. They kowtow three times to his portrait and then put it back in its place. They do the same before the sacred board and the tablet of Wanli Mama. They may lead

> into the courtyard a domesticated, but normally not yet ridden chestnut *tahe* (sacrificial) horse covered with a saddle cloth and make it stand still. The master of the household holds the brazier in his hands and circles the horse three times. The horse is then led away and the portrait of Wanli Mama removed. A drake is killed, cooked in front of the sacred tree – usually a nearby elm – and put on a plate as an offering to the tree. During the rites, another animal is killed, its gall bladder hung on the tree and its bones placed carefully under it.

On the night of the first day of the rite, the family worship before the sacred board. They first present the sacrificial offerings, light incense, and offer the sacrificial cakes. All family members and relatives then kneel down. The official in charge of cooking puts the sacrificial animal on a rectangular wooden platter, and the master of the house pours liquor into its ear. If the animal cries out and twitches its ear, people call this *lingsheng* (领牲, the sacrifice is accepted). Before the animal is slain, the master takes off his hat and kneels to it to express his gratitude. After the animal is slaughtered, its hair is removed, and its entrails and hooves are commonly dismembered into eight parts, cooked, and then offered to the gods. The different parts of the cooked meat are laid out to resemble the animal's whole body, which is placed on a sacrificial board, called *zu* (俎). With all lights extinguished, the master kneels down, gropes for a wine cup, takes it, and fills it with liquor. As junior members of the family stand attentively, he raises the cup above his head and passes it to three of them, signifying that descendants are drinking the liquor as substitutes for deceased ancestors. After that, the master delivers a speech in the Manchu language. Family members drum chopsticks on bowls in response and sing chants to present the sacrifice to the deities with great piety. After a while, the lights are relit, and all kneel down and kneel three more times. Finally, the sacrificial board is removed, and all gather to eat the meat. They put a little minced meat on the tin plate on top of the *somoimoo* to feed crows.

On the second day of the rite, the family worship the sacred pole, kill another sacrificial animal, skin it, singe its hair, cook it, divide up the meat, and then fry rice. They spread out a tarpaulin over the courtyard, and clan relatives all gather to eat the meat. Passers-by can also enjoy a share of the meat, and the host may give a slice of the roasted skin as a special token of respect. When the guests leave, they need not express gratitude, and the host need not see them off.

On the third day, people worship Wanli Mama. They take the five-coloured cords out of the pouch, leading them through the hall door and then tying them to the *somoimoo*. An animal sacrifice is offered and its meat cooked in the same way as the first night's worship before the sacred board. Afterwards, the *huansuo* ritual honouring the goddess of fertility Fodo Mama described in Chapter 3 is held. Unmarried boys and unmarried girls all kneel down in front of the tablet of Wanli Mama, and senior women dip willow twigs into clean water, sprinkle them over the unmarried ones, and put the coloured *huansuo* strings around their necks. After three days, the string chain is taken off and put back in the purse for use in the next sacrificial ritual. The married women let their husband's family prepare a pig and liquor to worship Wanli Mama while they preserve a new *huansuo* in that family.

Finally, a 1777 Qing work adds that "another Manchu tradition is to worship ancestors on the first day and fifteenth day of a lunar month, which is the same as the tradition of the Han Chinese."

The 1891 Qing work *Annals of Jilin* (*Jilin tongzhi*) describes Manchu sacrificial *jia* rites held by the common public of Jilin as follows:

> The Manchu rituals are magnificent. There is star worship and ancestor veneration as well as the spring and autumn *chunqiu* rituals (春秋祭) celebrating the revivification of nature in spring and the harvest in autumn. One day before these rites, people cook broomcorn millet, also known as glutinous millet, which they mash up and make into glutinous rice *dagao* cakes as sacrificial offerings, and clansmen visit one another. For the rite itself, a shaman puts on a sacred headdress and apron. In what is called dancing the family gods (*tiaojiashen*, 跳家神), he then dances, holding a drum and shaking his waist bells, and chants words to bring good fortune. The clansmen beat drums to echo the chant. During the ritual, they grind millet flour to make small wild mint cakes stuffed with bean-mash filling and wrapped with wild mint as offerings to the ancestors. The remaining procedures of the rite are the same as in *chunqiu* rituals. The Mongols offer pigs and sheep in sacrificial rituals similar to those of the Manchu. Because troubles and misfortunes often strike people, they sacrifice animals to seek blessings from the gods. They also hold sacrificial rituals at home on one's birthday or the anniversary of a loved one's death. They rarely build shrines.
>
> (Guobuluo Changshun 1989)

The *Annals of Jilin* continues as follows:

> The Manchu people, whether of high or low status, must worship deity tablets with no inscriptions in their homes. Some use wooden coffers instead of tablets. They place one tablet on the west wall and the other on the north wall of the principal room. For rooms with a southern or northern exposure, the west is regarded as the most sacred direction, but for rooms with an eastern or western exposure, the south is most sacred, and the shrine is placed on the south wall. Some families use yellow satin to make the shrine curtains. Others place a chair on the shrine of the north wall and under it place five pieces of wood sawed into the shape of a tablet; or they place there a stool and under it three pieces of wood, over which incense is sprinkled and burned during the rite. People select a spring or autumn day to hold the rite and perform a trance dance. They know little about the dance, but they think it is performed to worship the ancestors. Among all the deities worshipped, Avalokiteśvara comes first, then Guan Di, and then the god of the soil and the gnome-like god of the ground. People thus use three plates of incense.
>
> (Guobuluo Changshun 1989)

Before the rite, the pigs used in sacrifice must be pure black. They are placed in front of the gods before daybreak on the day of the rite. The officiant raises their cup of liquor to express respect for the pig, and then they pour it into the pig's ear. If the ear twitches, that is an auspicious sign. If it does not, it means that it is not pure black, the sacrificial utensils are not clean, or the fast is not sufficiently pious, and there will be baneful events. In that case, people have to kneel and pray again until the pig twitches its ear. After the pig has been cooked, its head, tail, shoulders, ribs, lungs, and heart are put on the sacrificial *zu* board, and a small amount of meat from each part is placed in a big copper bowl as *ama zunrou* (dish of meat honouring Nurhaci). People then offer the meat to the gods and kneel. The officiant stands in front, with other men standing behind him according to their clan seniority, and the women then line up behind the men, all with head coverings removed. All kneel. After the ritual, people gather before the gods and eat the *ama zunrou*, which symbolizes that they are receiving the meat as a blessing. At night, another animal is killed and sacrificed in the same manner as in the daytime ceremony. All lights are extinguished, and the sacrificial meat for this rite is called *bidengrou* (避灯肉), meat offered to the gods with all lights out. The meat sacrificed to gods must not be taken out of the home, but its bones are given to dogs. If they do not eat them all up, the remaining bones are left outdoors at night. Some families burn the remaining bones and then bury them, and they may give the *bidengrou* to friends and relatives. On the same day, the family serve guests with the meat, but after eating, the guests need not express their gratitude or the family see them off. Only when the guests and the host meet the next time can the guests express their thanks.

Turning from Jilin further north to Heilongjiang, the 1933 *Heilongjiang Annals* (*Heilongjiang zhigao*) describes Manchu sacrificial *jia* rituals in that province:

> People worship heaven and earth at daybreak of the second day, which is known as "fulfilling old vows" (还愿, *huanyuan*). A rectangular altar table is set up behind a screen wall in the courtyard, and three wooden cups and a plate of broomcorn millet are placed on it. A pig is skinned and divided into eleven parts, which are placed facing toward the east of the wall. A pot and brazier are put at the west of the wall, and a little meat is cooked, cut into small squares, and put into two porcelain pots. Two wooden bowls are filled with steamed millet and placed on the altar. The shaman goes down on one knee, chanting prayers. Holding copper spoons with the meat and millet, he then kowtows to the west and south respectively nine times. In the east corner of the courtyard a sacred *somomoo* is erected, which is, an ancestor pole with several *zhang* high, known as the pole of good fortune. At the top is fastened a tin dipper, or wood dipper for a poor family. When the family begins to worship the pole, they fill the dipper with the pig's tail and bladder, and also millet. The top of the pole is pointed, and on it the bones of the pig's neck are stuck horizontally for crows to eat. . . . It is said that crows once rescued Manchu ancestors when they were in danger, so people worship them for their

> kindness. It is also said that the pole is erected to worship heaven and as a means of communication with heaven. After worshipping the pole, people eat the remaining meat in the courtyard, which is known as "sharing the simple meat meal" (*chixiaoroufan*, 吃小肉饭). In the afternoon, the family stew the meat of the pig, singe its hair, and then eat the meat in their room, known as "sharing the great meat meal" (*chidaroufan*, 吃大肉饭). When the sun sets, people worship the Stars in front of the chimney of the east room. During the ceremony, a person dressed in white kneels on the ground with all lights and candles extinguished. When he finishes praying, he holds a wooden knife in his left hand and stabs the pig. Later he does so with a real knife. After the ceremony, friends and relatives are invited to share the meat, and when they finish eating, the lights or candles are lit again. A pure black pig must be used for the sacrifice, and the leftovers must be buried in the courtyard and the bones tossed into the river.
>
> (Heilongjiang Annals Editorial Committee 1992)

Usually the whole rite lasts two days, but in affluent households, it may continue for six or seven days. There are female shamans as well as male shamans, and the number of shamans invited varies according to the family's financial status. In the past, families would hold the *jia* ritual once a year or offer prayers on the winter solstice, but this is rarely seen nowadays. Some people pray to their ancestors, to protect them as they sail through troubles or recover from illness, and some worship the ancestors to express gratitude for their wealth, peace, or a happy event. They worship deity tablets or sacred wooden coffers indoors. If the house has a southern exposure, the west is regarded as the sacred direction; if it has an eastern or western exposure, the south is so regarded. Sacrificial rites must be held on auspicious days, and the sacrificial pig should be chosen on such a day. It must be pure black, and once chosen, it cannot be used for other purposes, even when the ritual is postponed for three or even five years.

In procedures similar to the rites just described, at dawn on the day of the sacrifice, the pig is led before the gods, and the officiant raises a wine cup and prays. People then pour liquor into the pig's ear. If it twitches, this indicates *lingsheng* (sacrifice accepted); if it does not, the officiant must pray again until *lingsheng* occurs. Afterwards, the pig is dismembered and cooked before the gods. Then people cut out small pieces of the pig's head, tail, shoulders, ribs, lungs and heart and put them on a bronze plate as the *ama zunrou* (dish of meat honoring Nurhaci). They set the plate before the gods, kneel three times, and offer it three times. The officiant and all clan members kneel down in rows according to seniority and kneel. After that, everyone goes before the gods and eats the meat as a sign that they share in its blessing. At night, they again offer sacrifice, the same as for the daytime ritual, but with the lights out, offering the sacrificial meat, called *bidengrou*. People eat it and then bury the leftovers. During the rite, invited shamans perform a dance. When the pig is sacrificed in the daytime rite, the shaman wears a sacred headdress; shakes their girdle bells; beats a drum while shaking their waist, hands, and feet; and chants a prayer to the sound of the drumbeats and tinkling of the waist bells. A pole is erected on the left side of the courtyard and a platelike tin dipper is tied to the top. People worship the pole and offer a sacrificial animal before it the following day in an action known as worshipping heaven. After the rite, the pig's chitterlings, lungs, tripe, and other parts are placed in the tin dipper to feed crows. If friends or relatives visit that day, they stay and use their knives to help themselves to some of the meat. When they finish eating, they need not express their thanks, and the host need not see them off.

The foregoing excerpts of Manchu shamanic rituals from Liaoling, Jilin, and Heilongjiang provide a basis for comparison and analysis. As is related in the records of these three provinces, the procedures of the Manchu *jia* folk ritual have much in common. In terms of preserving ancient Manchu beliefs, however, the Heilongjiang rite is more effective than that in Jilin, and the Jilin rite is more effective than that in Mukden (Shenyang, 沈阳) and the surrounding areas of Liaoning. Nonetheless, in 1984, a hundred years after the account in *Annals of Jilin*, I videotaped a Manchu *jia* ritual held by several clans in Yongji County of Jilin Province, which revealed that the traditional form of the rite has been well preserved there. As of the writing of this book, moreover, shamanic rituals, with complete sacred texts and traditional ritual instruments are still preserved among some Manchu clans in both Jilin and Heilongjiang, and new male and female clan shamans are still initiated to pass the rituals down. Furthermore, the gathering of *mukūn* (subclans) has been strictly preserved by the Guan clan in the town of Ula, Yongji County, and in Heilongjiang by the Zhao clan of Sanjiazi Village and the Li clan of Bohai, Ning'an County.

Among the Manchu rituals performed by the common people, along with *jia* rituals (*jiaji*,家祭), some clans still perform *dashen* rituals (*dashenji*,大神祭) and *ye* rituals (*yeji*, 野祭), with their powerful primitive religious overtones. In addition to the *jia* ritual procedures, which are quite similar among various Manchu clans, other ritual actions are necessary in these rites. For the *dashen* rite, for instance, people set up a *dashenanzi* (大神案子) altar board and a canvas with images of shaman deities, and shamans summon their clan's animal deities, bird deities, and other personified animal patron gods of land or water, as well as their ancestral gods and the Manni hero gods noted in Chapter 3. The Manchu worship more than thirty ancestral Manni (瞒尼) or Malu deities, including Amba Manni, Baturu Manni, Juru Manni, and so on, each with each deity's unique magical powers. The *dashen* rite is commonly performed by senior shamans, called *dashen* (大神, great spirits), who have special divine powers when possessed. They are aided by other shamans, and pooling their joint efforts, they use their special powers to summon, praise, entertain, and send the gods away.

The early-20th-century Chinese work by a Japanese spy agency, *Annals of All Provinces of the Republic of China* (*Zhonghuo minguo quanguo shengqu quanzhi*), gives the following information about *dashen* rites:

> The shaman's hat is like a helmet with a green brim and five colored pendulous strips and two small mirrors which look like eyes. The shaman's face

> is covered by slips of paper, and he or she wears a red costume and dances to loud drumbeats. The most powerful shamans can use mirrors to exorcise evil spirits and cure disease. They apply a mirror to the patient, and when it touches the diseased part, it sticks to it and cannot be easily removed. Once it vibrates, the bone joints make an echoing sound, and the patient recovers. The patient's family fashion a straw human being, bird, or beast, which is worshipped amid drumbeats and chanting and then sent off. The head of the straw figure is cut off and hung on a pole because people believe it can exorcise ghosts.
>
> (Lu Long and Bai Meichu 1924:48)

The same work continues as follows:

> Among all the shamans (*wu*巫), there are well-known *dashen*, who are usually young, and their assistant *ershen* (二神, secondary shamans). When a family holds a sacrificial ritual, a pig, liquor and incense are placed before the shamanic gods before they can be invited. The *dashen* wears his or her sacred outfit and hat. The hat and belt are decorated with small bells, and when the *dashen* is possessed by a god, he or she can dance continuously to the tinkling of the bells. After a while, all lights are extinguished. Once when the Manchu language was then heard spoken, it turned out that the possessed shaman was asking questions and the assistant was responding. Their voices were loud and distinct, with long, sweeping tones, much like those of folk songs. The *dashen* first chanted and then the *ershen* and other people repeated the last notes together and beat their drums. Then the rite was over.
>
> (Lu Long and Bai Meichu 1924:48)

Such documents about past *dashen* rites can be found among many Manchu clans, and we have documents for some clans that describe the rituals for ye spirits (animal spirits,野神).[3] The ye spirits and plant deities preserved in some clans can be as many as thirty or forty, and there are numerous ancient ancestral shaman gods and hero gods worshipped in each clan as well, in some clans reaching a hundred. After the Liberation of China in 1949, a few clans that have still preserved shamanic rituals and the sacred ritual texts, and instruments, and they still have people who can perform *dashen* rituals. However, most clans preserve the sacred texts but no longer have shamans, while some still have shamans but have lost their texts and ritual instruments.

6.3 Shamanic rituals of the Oroqen, Ewenki, Daur, and Hezhe

Extensive investigations into the last decades of the 20th century found shamans still alive among the Oroqen, Ewenki, Daur, Mongols, and other ethnic groups. Two senior Oroqen shamans in the Greater Khingan Range region, Heilongjiang, had sacred instruments and could cure diseases for their clanspeople. There were also two shamans in the Hulun Buir, Inner Mongolia. However, a venerable female Daur shaman passed away in 1988, and surveys reveal that shaman rites have been going extinct among these ethnic peoples. Most examples of shamanic activity are limited to written statements dating from the mid 20th century and are neither detailed nor ample in comparison with what can be found among the Manchu. Of the Hezhe in Tongjiang City of eastern Heilongjiang, You Jinliang (尤金良) once said that their shamans have long been extinct and that none exist anymore. He noted that there are only some oral tales and legends about shamans preserved by elderly Hezhe. As for the Xibe, evidence of their shamanic activities has been preserved mainly in the Qapqal Xibe autonomous county, Xinjiang. The *Shaman Songs* (*Saman sheng*e) collected and released towards the end of the 20th century was originally preserved by ordinary Xibe people and are significant for the research of their shamanic culture and folk customs and for their general history.

I have learned, however, that shamanism still prevails among the Mongols of eastern Inner Mongolia and that some rituals are still practised there, especially those centred on *ovoo*, the stone cairns on mountain tops and road passes. These cairns originally served as landmarks, but later Mongols and related peoples came to regard them as religious markers for the worship of the god of heaven, mountain gods, road gods, and other nature and ancestral deities. They serve as a sacrificial altar in the shape of a mound, usually made from piles of rocks. If no rocks are available, people weave willow branches into baskets and stuff soil inside them. The basket is round with a spire and is usually placed on a small mound. There are large and small *ovoo*, and sometimes, several small *ovoo* are put near or in front of a big one. In the middle is stuck a wooden pole, three to four *zhang* in height. Numerous square cloths with scriptures written on them festoon the pole. *Ovoo* worship is deeply rooted in Mongol culture and sincerely respected by the people. Before they set out on a long journey, they pick up a stone from an *ovoo* and carry it with them, hoping that they can thus be safe and sound throughout the journey. When they encounter an *ovoo* on their way, they kneel and then walk around it. When horse riders come across one, they dismount and worship before it. *Ovoo* worship is held regularly every year, moreover, among which the autumn ritual is the most majestic. The present midsummer Nadam Fair held throughout the country, with its wrestling, horse racing, and archery games, has its roots in *ovoo* worship.

Among the Oroqen, the primary purpose for the religious activities practised by their shamans is to pray for and bless diseased loved ones and conduct prayers for a bounteous hunt or harvest. Shamans who treat patients of their clan are called *bakci*, and the deities who possess them are the nature deities Jiyaci, Jolo Borukan, Hulujin Hadar, Kutun Borukan, and other goddesses. There is only one *bakci* in a *mukūn*, and some *mukūn* do not have a *bakci*. When they are treating patients, *bakci* do not wear a special sacred outfit or sit on a sacred stool. Rather, they sit on a *malu*, the place of honour facing the door. They treat the patient after being possessed by one of the numerous deities worshipped in Oroqen shamanism. Apart from the ancient nature deities just mentioned, there are deities who have care of various diseases, such as the goddess Ergudun for smallpox, Deleku Daryir for convulsions, Urenhadar for medical exanimations, and Ercin for headaches and chest pains. There are also deities in charge of hunting and production, such as Jiyaci, who is worshipped when hunters have long been unable to track down an animal.

The Daur also worship numerous deities. Hunters worship the mountain god Bainaca, and foresters and fishers the river god Birgebal. Everyone worships *ovoo* and Tengri, the heaven god or sky god. On the whole, their deities can be divided into two categories: those that have long been worshipped in one's clan and those that were introduced from other clans. Deities are worshipped in the form of idols. When a clansperson falls ill, a cow, sheep, pig, or chicken is sacrificed, and their shaman-like *yadegen* conducts prayers and performs a trance dance to expel the disease. Shamans who have long served their *mukūn* are highly respected. As of the writing of this book, Jin Mokun of a village in Qiqihar was the youngest clan shaman. In addition to treating illness, *yadegen* perform bone setting, help deliver babies, and offer the blood and meat of sacrificial animals to express gratitude to the gods. They also seek to satisfy ghosts in prayerful activities known as *baitelebei* (pray). In past times, shamans would summon the blue and white python god, the black and white fox goddess, pairs of male and female mad wolves, and the ferocious black bear. During the trance dance, the shamans demonstrate various skills: *zouzhadao* (走铡刀, walking on knives); *tiaotiexie* (跳铁鞋, applying wax or oil to one's feet and then leaping about on red-hot ploughshares); *jiehongdai* (结红带, entwining a red-hot iron chain around one's bared waist), *zouhuochi* (走火池, running over burning coals); *shetian hongyundou* (舌舔红熨斗, licking a red-hot iron with one's tongue), and *fan'gunshimo* (翻滚石磨, tossing a millstone).

Daur shamans regularly hold three types of clan rituals: *jieshen* (洁身, purification), *yirdeng*, and *ominan*. The third is the most ceremonious. Held in the third or fourth lunar month every three years, it consists of sacrifice to the gods. The officiant, who is always a new shaman, commonly performs a trance dance in a home or near the village. The rite lasts for three days, and on midnight of the third day, the blood-drinking *shaxue* (歃血) rite is held, in which the gods are offered in a *tan'gula* birch bark bowl a mixture of ox blood, ox milk, milk wine, nine bits of incense, and nine portions of ox lung. With all the lights extinguished, the shaman beats a drum, dances up and down, and mimics the cry of a cuckoo. All those present simultaneously echo and imitate the shaman. Afterwards, the lights are reignited and ox blood smeared on the mouth of every spirit idol. With this, the *ominan* rite is over.

Ewenki shamans are hereditary and enjoy high prestige among the people. All take part in the grand *ominarang* rite held in August, when lambs are weaned. They all wear their shamanic garb, but only one shaman is masked. All the participants contribute their sheep, chickens, and milk for a large communal ritual meal. The women are in charge of cooking, usually using more than twenty pots and pans. For the ritual, twenty or thirty people clasp their hands and form a circle, swaying and dancing. The shamans and elders sing songs and perform trance dances together for three days and nights, playing around the clock, with assistants helping the shamans with their singing.

Ewenki shamans also perform a trance dance to treat patients, and when people worship heaven or worship the nature god Jiyaci in the spring and autumn, shamans are invited to sing chants to seek blessings for peace and fruitful stock breeding. They are also invited to conduct prayers if someone has an inauspicious dream or suffers a great loss in stock breeding. When they treat an illness by exorcising an unsettled spirit, a black goat is slaughtered or, for a large-scale trance dance, a yearling calf, which is then given to the shaman after the ritual. The animal is needed for the spirit ghost to ride after the trance.

In the past, Hezhe shamans would perform *tiaolushen* (跳鹿神, leaping the deer god) every February and March and also in July and August, when it is known as *tiaotaipingshen* (跳太平神, leaping the god of peace). In this rite, people pray to the gods in the hope of expelling ill fortune and being blessed with good fortune. A shaman divines the date for the rite, and on that date, after the sun has climbed to a height of three bamboo poles, they take the Aimi god and sacred instruments out of a pack and place them on the west *kang*. The shaman then burns incense, offers food and liquor, and worships before the gods. When the various deities descend, clanspeople sprinkle liquor on the shaman, and young men of the village take sacred wands and deity figurines and beat drums as they follow the shaman out of the house, singing and dancing. Filing in formation, family by family, they place the Aimi god under the *kang*, put a sacred eagle on the *kang*, and stick a sacred knife in front of the west *kang*, with its sharp point downwards and knife edge outward. All the while, the shaman performs a trance dance outside the house door and then in the west room. All is repeated three times. Then the group line up and set off to another house. The number of families they visit should be odd – seven, nine, or eleven, and so on – and every family has to propose a toast to the shaman. When the shaman reaches the last family, they take off the shaman dress, rest, and are treated by the host. They then put the ritual dress back on, and clanspeople sprinkle liquor on the shaman. All the way back home, the shaman chants spirit songs and upon reaching home circles the house three times before entering. Afterwards, the shaman goes to the sacred pole, and people who have fulfilled their vows or are to make vows gather in front of the pole, offering sacrifice and praying.

In the past, the Hezhe also worshipped the god of heaven in the form of a spirit idol placed in a sacred tree. They also worshipped the auspicious star god with a *jia* ritual, and they did the same for the tree god when they set off for a hunt or returned from it. Among their numerous deities, they also worshipped their ancestor gods, placing the ancestral spirit idols on the west *kang*, burning incense, offering liquor in sacrifice, and kneeling. However, women were not allowed to attend this rite.

Notes

1 The deities are Ahun Nianxi, Anchu Ayala, Muri Muriha, Nadan Daihūn, Narhvn Hiyancu, Enduri Sengge, Baiman Janggin, Nadan Weihuri, Endu Monggolo, and Katun Noyan.

2 The eight Manchu banners were the yellow banner, white banner, red banner, blue banner, bordered yellow banner, bordered white banner, bordered red banner, and bordered blue banner. Along with the Han Army Eight Banners and Mongolian Eight Banners, they formed the military backbone of the Qing dynasty.

3 They are found, for example, in the Nimaca Hala, Diaoluo Hala, Hexeri Hala, Siheteli Hala, Namduru Hala, Kūyala Hala, Wuhuguae, Nimaca Hala, Diaoluo Hala, and Hexeri.

Bibliography

Akamatsu Chijyo赤松智诚1938. *Chaoxian wushu de yanjiu*朝鲜巫术的研究 [A Study of Korean Shamanism]. Osaka: Osaka House Bookstore.

Arsenyev, B.K. 1983. *Lin zhong ren wudehe*林中人–乌德赫[Udege in the Forest]. Trans. Guo Yanshun郭燕顺 and Sun Yunlai孙运来. *Minzu yiwenj* 民族译文集 [A Collection of Translated Ethnic Essays]. Changchun: Jilin Social Sciences Press吉林社会科学院出版社.

Bai Chunyi 白纯义and Yu Fengtong于凤桐1927. *Huinan xianzhi*辉南县志 [Huinan Annals]. Press unknown.

Ban Gu班固 (Eastern Han Dynasty) 1985. *Baihutong*白虎通. [Compilation of Conference Materials on the Confucian Classics in the Eastern Han Dynasty]. Beijing: Shanghai Commercial Press商务印书馆.

Bo Shaobu 波少布 1987. "*Duokeduo'er shan jidian yishi yanjiu* 多克多尔山祭奠仪式研究 [Research on the Sacrificial Ritual of Dokdor Mountain]." *Heilongjiang minzn congkan*黑龙江民族丛刊 [Heilongjiang Ethnic Series]. Harbin: Heilongjiang Institute of Ethnology黑龙江省民族研究所.

Cai Jiaqi蔡家麒1988. *Lun yuanshi zongjiao* 论原始宗教 [Primordial Religion]. Kunming: Yunnan Ethnic Publishing House云南民族出版社.

Cao Tingjie曹廷杰1934. *Xiboliyadongpian jiyao*西伯利亚东偏纪要 [Records of Eastern Siberia]. Shengyang: Liaohai Book Press辽海书社.

Cui Gaowei 崔高维 1987. *Heilongjiang yan'an de buluo* 黑龙江沿岸的部落 *[The Tribes along Heilong River].* Changchun: Jilin Culture and History Press吉林文史出版社.

——— 1997. *Zhouli yili*周礼·仪礼 [Rites of Zhou: Etiquette]. Shengyang: Liaoning Education Press辽宁教育出版社.

Ding Shan丁山1988. *Zhongguo gudai zongjiao yu shenhuakao*中国古代宗教与神话考[Investigations on Chinese Ancient Religion and Mythology]. Shanghai: Shanghai Literature and Art Publishing House上海文艺出版社.

Fan Ye 范晔 (Southern Song Dynasty) 1965. *Houhan shu*后汉书 [Book of Later Han]. Beijing: Zhonghua Book Company中华书局.

Fang Xuanling房玄龄 (Tang Dynasty) 1974. *Ji shu*晋书 [Book of Jin]. Beijing: Zhonghua Book Company中华书局.

Fu Yuguang富育光1984. *Qicai shenhuo*七彩神火 [Seven-hued Divine Fire]. Changchun: Jilin People's Publishing House吉林人民出版社.

——— 2007. *Donghai chenyuan lu*东海沉冤录 [Records of Grievances of the East Sea]. Changchun: Jilin People's Publishing House吉林人民出版社.

——— and Jing Wenli荆文礼2009. *Tiangong dazhan*天宫大战 [War in Heaven]. Changchun: Jilin People's Publishing House吉林人民出版社.

——— and Lu Liankun鲁连坤2007. *Wubuxiben mama*乌布西奔妈妈 [Umesiben Mama]. Changchun: Jinlin People's Publishing House 吉林人民出版社.

Guo Xileng郭熙楞1914. *Jinlin huizheng*吉林汇徵 [Collected Records of Jilin]. Press unknown.

Guo Yanshun 郭燕顺and Sun Yunlai 孙运来1983. "*Aiwenkeren*埃文基人[The Evenki]." *Minzu yiwenji* 民族译文集 [A Collection of Translated Ethnic Essays]. Changchun: Jilin Academy of Social Sciences 吉林省社会科学院.

Guobuluo Changshun郭布罗长顺 (Qing Dynasty) et al. 1989. *Jilin tongzhi*吉林通志 [Annals of Jilin]. Changchun: Jilin Culture and History Press吉林文史出版社.

He Ling 贺灵1990. "*Xibozu Xinyang de samanjiao gaikuang*锡伯族信仰的萨满教概况 [Survey of Xibe Shamanism]." *Samanjiao wenhua yanjiu* 萨满教文化研究 [Studies on Shaman Cultures]. Vol. 1. Changchun: Jilin People's Publishing House吉林人民出版社.

Heilongjiang Annals Editorial Committee黑龙江志稿编委会1992. *Heilongjiang zhigao* 黑龙江志稿 [Heilongjiang Annals]. Harbin: Heilongjiang People's Publishing House 黑龙江人民出版社.

Heine, Heinrich 1974. *Lun deguo zongjiao he zhexue de lishi*论德国宗教和哲学的历史 [History of Religion and Philosophy in Germany]. Beijing: Commercial Press商务印书馆.

Hong Hao洪皓 (Southern Song Dynasty) 1868. *Songmo jiwen*松莫纪闻 [Records of Songmo]. Beijing: The Four Imperial Libraries四库馆.

Hu Pu'an 胡朴安1986. *Zhonghua quanguo fengsuzhi*中华全国风俗志 [Social Life and Customs in China]. Shijiazhuang: Hebei People's Publishing House 河北人民出版社.

Inan, Abdülkadir 1979. *Samanjiao jinxi*萨满教今昔 [Shamanism in History and Today]. Trans. Yao Guomin姚国民and Zeng Xianying曾宪英. Beijing: Institute for Ethnic Literatre in Chinese Academy of Social Sciences中国社会科学院民族文学研究所.

Inner Mongolia Editorial Committe内蒙古自治区编委会 1986a. *Ewenkezu shehui lishi tiaocha baogao*鄂温克族社会历史调查报告 [Sociohistorical Investigation on the Evenki]. Hohhot: Inner Mongolia People's Publishing House内蒙古人民出版社.

——— 1986b. *Dawo'erzu shehui lishi tiaocha baogao*达斡尔族社会历史调查报告 [Sociohistorical Investigation on the Daur]. Hohhot: Inner Mongolia People's Publishing House内蒙古人民出版社.

——— 1986c. *Elunchuzu shehui lishi tiaocha baogao* 鄂伦春族社会历史调查报告 [Sociohistorical Investigation on the Oroqen]. Hohhot: Inner Mongolia People's Publishing House内蒙古人民出版社.

Ivanov, C.B. 1990. *Guidebook of Ethnic Plastic Arts in the Amur River Basin* [*Heilongjiang liuyu minzu yishu zaoxing shouce*黑龙江流域民族造型艺术手册]. Trans. Sun Yunlai 孙运来. Tianjin: Tianjin Classics Publishing House天津古籍出版社.

Jilin Archaeological Research Office吉林省考古研究室1975. *Xiboliya de gudai wenhua* 西伯利亚的古代文化 [Ancient Peoples of Siberia and their Cultures]. Changchun: Jilin Archaeological Research Office吉林省考古研究室.

Jin Qicong金启孮 trans. 1986. "*Xiboliya ge minzu zhi samanjiao*西伯利亚各民族之萨满教 [Shamanism of the Siberian Peoples]." *Samanjiao ziliao yanjiu cankao ziliao*萨满教研究参考资料[Reference Materials for Shaman Studies]. Vol. 1. Beijing: Institute of Ethnology, Chinese Academy of Social Sciences中国社会科学院民族研究所.

La Fargue, Paul 1963. *Zongjiao yu ziben*宗教与资本 [Religion and Capital]. Trans. Wang Ziye王子野. Shanghai: Joint Publishing Company 三联书店.

Li Di李迪1986. "*Mengguzu zaoqi de tianxiangguan*蒙古族早期的天象观 [Early Celestial Concepts of the Mongols]." *Neimenggu shehuikexue*内蒙古社会科学 [Inner Mongolia

Social Science]. Vol. 4. Hohhot: Inner Mongolia Academy of Social Sciences内蒙古自治区社会科学院.

Li Jiancai 李健才1986. *Dongbei shidi kaolue*东北史地考略 [Brief Introduciton to Archaeological Sites in Northeast China]. Changchun: Jilin People's Publishing House吉林人民出版社.

Li Jiarui李家瑞1992. *Beiping fengsu leizheng*北平风俗类徵 [Collected Customs of Beiping]. Beijing: Commercial Press商务印书馆.

Li Shutian李树田1987. *Changbaishan huigang zhilue*长白山汇岗志略 [Introduction to the Annals of Changbai Mountain]. Changchu: Jilin Culture and History Press吉林文史出版社.

Liu Jianguo刘建国1981. "*Guanyu samanjiao de jige wenti*关于萨满教的几个问题 [Questions about Shamanism]." *Shijie zongjiao yanjiu*世界宗教研究 [Studies on World Religions]. Vol. 2. Beijing: Institute for World Religions, Chinese Academy of Social Sciences中国社会科学院世界宗教研究所.

Liu Xin 刘歆 (Han Dynasty) 1989. *Shanhaijing*山海经 [Classic of Mountains and Seas]. Annotated by Guo Pu 郭璞. Shanghai: Shanghai Classics Publishing House上海古籍出版社.

Longjiang Annals Editorial Committee 1991. *Longjiang xianzhi*龙江县志[Longjiang Annals]. Beijing: Chinese City Press中国城市出版社.

Lu Long卢龙and Bai Meichu白眉初1924. *Zhonghua minguo quanguo shengqu quanzhi*中华民国全国省区全志 [Annals of All Provinces of the Republic of China]. Vol. 3. Beijing: Beijing Normal University Press 北京师范大学出版社

*Manzhou shilu*满洲实录 [Veritable Records of the Manchu] 1986. Beijing: Zhonghua Book Company中华书局.

Mao Dun 茅盾1929. *Shenhua zalun*神话杂论[Miscellaneous Mythic Studies]. Shanghai: Shanghai World Book Company上海世界书局.

Ning'an Annals Editorial Committee宁安县志编委员会1989. *Ning'an Xianzhi*宁安县志 [Ning'an Annals]. Harbin: Heilongjiang People's Publishing House黑龙江人民出版社.

Pan Rongbi潘荣陛 (Qing Dynasty) 1981. *Yanjing suishiji*燕京岁时记 [Records of Seasonal Yanjing Customs]. Beijing: Beijing Classics Publishing House北京古籍出版社.

Peng Bo彭勃1996. *Manzu*满族 [The Manchu]. Chengdu: Sichuan Ethnic Publishing House四川民族出版社.

*Qingtaizu nupanyachi shilu*清太祖努尔哈赤实录 [Veritable Records of the Qing Emperor Nurhaci] 1989. Shanghai: Shanghai Bookstore 上海书店.

Qiu Pu秋浦1962. *Ewenkeren de yuanshi shehui xingtai*鄂温克人的原始社会形态[Primordial Social Forms of the Ewenki]. Beijing: Zhonghua Book Company中华书局.华书局.

——— 1985. *Samanjiao yanjiu*萨满教研究 [Studies of Shamanism]. Shanghai: Shanghai People's Publishing House 上海人民出版社.

Schmidt, Wilhelm 1987. *Yuanshi zongjiao yu shenhua*原始宗教与神话 [The Origin and Growth of Religion]. Trans. Xiao Shiyi萧师毅 and Chen Xiangchun 陈祥春. Shanghai: Shanghai literature and Art Publishing House上海文艺出版社.

Shuangcheng Annals Editorial Committee双城县志编委会1990. *Shuangcheng xianzhi*双城县志 [Shuangcheng Annals]. Beijing: China Prospect Publishing House中国展望出版社.

Song Lian宋濂 (Ming Dynasty) 1975. *Yuanshi*元史 [History of Yuan]. Beijing: Zhonghua Book Company中华书局.

Sun, Y.A. and Li, X.R. 2004. "Study of *qi*, Systematic Function, and Materiality." *Chinese Journal of Basic Medicine in Traditional Chinese Medicine*. 10 (1).

Tangyuan Annals Editorial Committee汤原县地方志编纂委员会1992. Tangyuan xianzhi汤原县志 [Tangyuan Annals]. Harbin: Heilongjiang People's Publishing House黑龙江人民出版社.

Tsendin Damdinsüren策・达木丁苏伦1956. *Menggu mishi*蒙古秘史 [Secret History of the Mongols]. Bejing: Zhonghua Book Company中华书局.

Tuotuo 脱脱 (Toqto'a) et al. (Yuan Dynasty) 1974. *Liaoshi lizhi suichuyi* 辽史·礼志·岁除仪 [History of Liao: Treatises of Rituals, Ritual on the Eve of the Spring Festival]. Beijing: Zhonghua Book Company中华书局.华书局.

——— 1975. *Jinshi dilizhi* 金史地理志 [History of Jin: Treatise on Geography]. Beijing: Zhonghua Book Company中华书局.

Wang Chong王充 (Eastern Han Dynasty) 1974. *Lunhen*论衡 [Critical Essays]. Shanghai: Shanghai People's Publishing House 上海人民出版社.

Wei Shenghe魏声和et al. 1986. *Jilin liuwen lu* 吉林旧闻录 [Old Jilin Records]. Changchun: Jilin Culture and History Press吉林文史出版社.

Wu Yisang 吴依桑 and Bagen 巴根1987. "*Mengguzu baihuo xisu gaiguan*蒙古族拜火习俗概观 [Mongol Fire Rituals]." *Heilongjiang minzu congkan* 黑龙江民族丛刊 [Heilongjiang Ethnic Series]. Vol. 4. Harbin: Heilongjiang Institute of Ethnology黑龙江省民族研究所.

Xi Qing西清 (Qing Dynasty) 1984. *Heilongjiang waiji*黑龙江外记 [Records of beyond Heilongjiang]. Harbin: Heilongjiang People's Publishing House 黑龙江人民出版社.

Xiao Shi萧奭 (Qing Dynasty) 1997. *Yongxianlu*永宪录 [Records of Yongxian]. Beijing: ZhonghuaBook Company中华书局.

Xu Ke徐珂 (Qing Dynasty) 1984. *Qingbai leichao*清稗类抄 [Classified Qing Anecdotes]. Beijing: Zhonghua Book Company中华书局.

Xu Mengshen 徐梦莘 (Southern Song Dynasty) 1987. *Sanchaobeimeng huibian*三朝北盟会编 [Documents of the Three Reigns' Northern Alliance]. Vol. 3. Shanghai: Shanghai Classics Publishing House上海古籍出版社.

Yang Bin杨宾 (Qing Dynasty) et al. 1985. *Ningguta jilue*宁古塔纪略 [Summary Records of Ningguta]. Harbin: Heilongjiang People's Publishing House 黑龙江人民出版社.

Ye Longli叶隆礼 (Song Dynasty) 1985. *Qidan guozhi*契丹国志 [Khitan Chronicles]. Annotated by Jia Jingyan贾敬颜and Lin Ronggui林荣贵. Shanghai. Shanghai Classics Publishing House上海古籍出版社.

Zhang Fengtai 张凤台 and Liu Longguang 刘龙光1910. *Changbai zhengcun lu*长白征存录 [Collected Records of Changbai Mountain]. Unpublished Manuscript.

Zhao Hui昭槤 (Qing Dynasty) 1980. *Xiaoting zalu*啸亭杂录 [Miscellaneous Records of Xiaoting]. Beijing: Zhonghua Book Company中华书局.

Zhen Jun震钧 (Qing Dynasty) 1982. *Tianzhi ouwen*天咫偶闻 [News from Heaven]. Beijing: Beijing Classics Publishing House北京古籍出版社.

Index